Ierusalem
hierosolima, coelestis ac ueri numinis cognitio, cultusq́, erant celeberrimi tepli menia. Hec hierosolima longe clarissima urbium ori
das
TAB.
& primu idioma permansit)ea esse, JERUSALEM. M.D.X. auctius & illustrius
DEAD SEA. GERARDUM raperet Magnum cum Parca maligna, nimis
and dedicated to the ri
the Sunne newly corrected. nullam ciuitate patribus olim Abrahę, Ysaac, & Iacob promissa 1595.
Sodom solimæ. q
Ierich
ABRAHAM the Patriarke.
RACCOLTO GIA
good Nauigation Campus
DOVZE TRIBVS D'ISRAEL
& del paese del Prete Elaths
à numine esset, terram uidelicet lacte & melle fluentem.
MARE MORTUUM LIBRORVM Evulgatas
PALÄSTINA
Rosso insino a Calicut, et all is
at the three Cranes in the Vinetree Qui terram & totum rimatus mente profundum
attorno il Mondo Luxi, illum raperet cùm fera Parca uirum:
Navigation.
The PEREGRINATION
HONDIUS ATLANTIS Ierusalem Mundi. lector optime, iniuria aut iactantia pura.

JOURNEYS TO THE PROMISED LAND

JOURNEYS TO THE PROMISED LAND

THE LAND OF ISRAEL

ANCIENT MAPS, PRINTS AND TRAVELOGUES THROUGH THE CENTURIES

PORTLAND HOUSE, NEW YORK

Editor: Nachman Ran
Adviser: Naftali Kadmon
Professor of Cartography,
Hebrew University of Jerusalem
Assist. Editor: Niva Panai
Production Manager: Gil Ran

Design: Frederic Gozlan

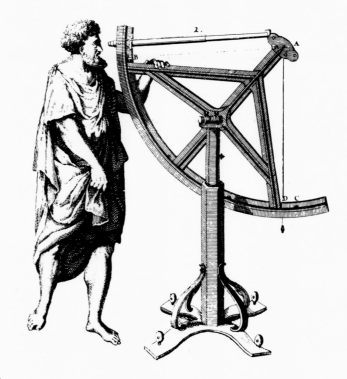

Sources, Photo Credits, Acknowledgments:

Am-Oved Publishing, Tel-Aviv: *p. 115;* American Museum, Madrid: *p. 88;* Ben-Gurion Residence, Tel-Aviv: *p. 132;* Bible Society, London: *p. 22, 23, 26, 34, 77;* Bibliothèque Municipale, Cambrai: *p. 31 (Ms.292);* Bibliothèque du Ministère des Armées, Paris: *p. 68;* Bibliothèque Nationale, Paris: *p. 23, 28, 39, 42, 59, 88;* Bibliothèque Royale, Bruxelles: *p. 67;* Bibliothèque Municipale, Boulogne-sur-mer: *p. 75 (Ms.188);* Bodleian Library, Oxford: *p. 65 (Ms. Laud.Or.234, fol.7v);* British Library, London: *p.34, 56 (Ms.Add.28681), 62 (Ms.Or.Royal 14C.), 71;* Chateau de Versailles: *p. 114, 115, 117;* Collection Giovanna, Firenze: *p. 88;* Dept. of Antiquities, Ministry of Education, Jerusalem: *p.44, 50, 75;* Dept. of Survey, Tel Aviv: *p. 48, 49, 122;* Ebstorf Museum, Lüneburg: *p. 60;* Freeman J., London: *p. 30, 31, 104;* Harris David, Jerusalem: *p. 51, 119;* Helikon Kiado, Budapest: *p. 65;* Holland Press, London: *p. 73;* Huntington Library, San Marino, California: *p. 25, 27, 92;* Israel Museum, Jerusalem: *p. 51, 119;* Kedar M., Jerusalem: *p. 36;* Koninklijke Bibliotheek, Den Haag: *p. 52 (Ms.76F5, fol.1r);* Library of Academy of Sciences, Budapest: *p. 65 (Ms.A77/I-IV);* Library of Stuttgart: *p. 67;* Musée Condé, Chantilly: *p. 39 (Ms.776), 75 (Ms.700), 115;* Musée des Beaux-Arts, Tours: *p. 79;* National Archives, Map Collection, Ottawa, Canada: *p. 100, 101;* National Maritime Museum, Haifa: *p. 84, 88, 89, 96, 97, 100, 101, 110, 118;* Photographie Giraudon-Lauros-Telarci, Paris: *p. 23, 28, 31, 39, 42, 47, 49, 75, 79, 88, 114, 115, 117;* Radovan Zeev, Jerusalem: *p. 50, 51;* Shocken Institute of the Jewish Theological Seminary of America, Jerusalem: *p. 20;* Shor N., Zahala: *p. 115;* Staats und Universitäts-Bibliothek, Hamburg: *p. 34 (Cod.Levy 22);* Zionist Archives, Jewish Agency, Jerusalem: *p. 124, 126, 127, 129, 130, 131.*

Journeys To The Promised Land was originally published in 1987 by Terra Sancta Arts.

This edition published by Portland House, a division of dilithium Press, Ltd., distributed by Crown Publishers, Inc., 225 Park Avenue South, New York, New York 10003. First published 1989 in Great Britain by Studio Editions an imprint of Bestseller Publications Ltd., Princess House, 50 Eastcastle Street, London W1N 7AP, England.

Copyright © Nachman Ran/Terra Sancta Arts, 1987.
ISBN 1-517-68916-2. Printed and bound in Hong Kong   hgfedcba

And Joshua charged them that went to describe the land, saying, Go and walk through the land, and describe it, and come again to me, that I may here cast lots for your before the LORD in Shi-loh.

And the men went and passed through the land, and described it by cities into seven parts in a book, and came again to Joshua to the host at Shi-loh.

Joshua 18:8,9

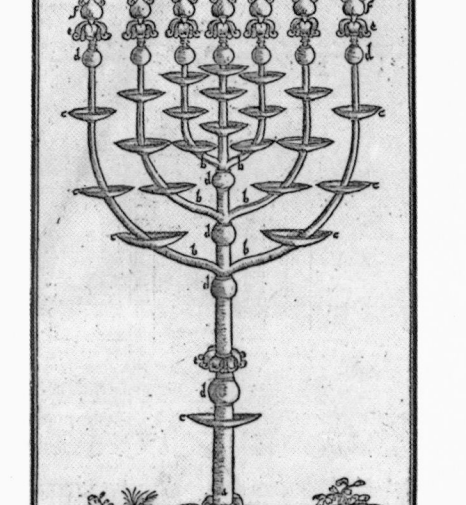

Contents

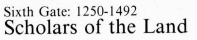

Preface

The well-known saying "all roads lead to Rome" is not, historically speaking, accurate. At best it might have been valid for the time of the Roman Empire. The historical truth is, in effect, that "all roads lead to Jerusalem" – from Abraham the Patriarch to this day – for almost four thousand years.

The roads and tracks to Jerusalem and to the Land of Israel have been covered over the generations by travellers and armies, individuals and groups. They came by sea and over land: Jews, Christians and Moslems. Jews who came to the land of their yearnings to pay their respects. Others who came to fortify their faith or to seize the land from their adversaries. Others still who came to travel through the land from end to end. For the most part, and in every era, these people have left their mark and their impressions – by pen or brush – by buildings, walls, or by their tombstones.

The literary harvest of the pilgrims who visited Jerusalem and the Land of Israel, who wrote about the land and studied it, totals some three thousand essays – a vast treasure-trove of knowledge. This contribution towards documenting the land, its history, researching its past, is of infinite importance.

When the age of discovering and exploring new continents had passed in Europe, it became necessary to document these discoveries, and the atlas began to flourish. Atlases were produced in many languages and in many countries, and they all boasted a map of the Land of Israel. At first these maps were purely of an illustrational nature, depicting the stories of the Bible, reconstructing the wanderings of the Israelites in the wilderness, and the division of the land into tribal portions. In time special maps of the Land of Israel were prepared for the use of Christian pilgrims.

This book spreads out before the reader a rich selection of travels to the Land of Israel from the time of Abraham the Patriarch to modern days and the realization of the Zionist dream. Each period and every pilgrimage is faithfully and impressively represented by the accounts of its participants, by maps and illustrations.

This is not a book of the history of the Land of Israel in the ordinary sense of the term, nor does it go into the various Jewish waves of immigration to this country or into the Moslem chapter of its history. These are well worth including in the next edition. This is first and foremost an art book, concentrating on travels along the tracks to the Land of Israel over the generations.

The resplendent design of this book makes it a very special work in the field of art literature. It will without a doubt enhance the collection of everyone interested in the history and art of the Land of Israel. Truly a superior wine in a choice vessel!

Yitzhak Navon
Deputy Prime Minister
and Minister for Education and Culture

Jerusalem, 1987

Foreword

Th is book has presented the editor with no little difficulty, deriving from the wealth of varied and diversified material existing on this subject. It would be virtually impossible to submit the entirety of this material to the interested reader. In this book, therefore, we have included only a minute quantity of the enormous mass of ancient maps of the Holy Land and of the travel accounts and pilgrimages.

Some 6000 maps referring to the Land of Israel have been produced in the last seven hundred years. They have appeared in the form of illustrations in manuscripts and books, mainly holy writings, within atlases and map collections. They were attached to essays written by pilgrims, since many travellers and pilgrims recounted their experiences and impressions of their visit to the Holy Land in writing.

From all this volume of material we have chosen the maps and personages which best characterize their respective times and convey to the reader some idea of the two main issues dealt with by this book: ancient maps and prints of the Holy Land, and travelogues through the centuries.

The book is divided into ten "gates" covering ten historical periods. In every gate it has been our wish to familiarize the reader with the notable men who visited the Holy Land and left their imprint on it. In each case we have added a map of the land closely linked to the activities of these men and their times.

Further appended to each gate are illustrations reflecting noteworthy actions or events which occurred during a respective period and remain enshrined in its history.

We take pleasure in expressing our grateful thanks to all the many research institutes, museums and libraries who assisted us in obtaining the reference and illustrative material for this book.

Nachman Ran
Editor

August, 1987

11

Introduction

by Naftali Kadmon

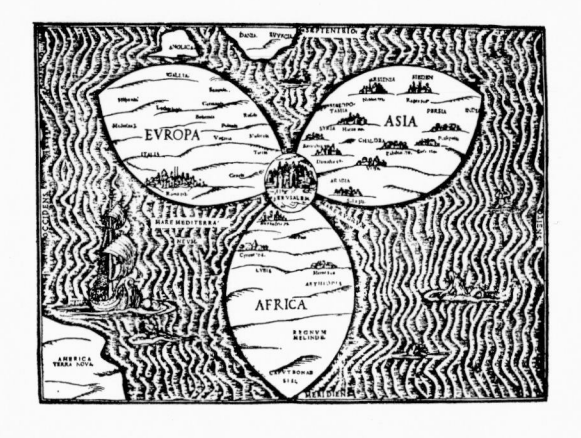

Few countries on earth display a diversity of landforms and climate within such a small space as does the Holy Land. Fewer still have attracted the attention of the world – and travellers from all countries – to the same extent. Two cultural centres developed in the ancient Middle East: one in Egypt, along the River Nile, and the other in Mesopotamia, between the Euphrates and the Tigris. Joining these countries along the relatively narrow belt of arable soil bordering the Mediterranean Sea has resulted in a settled region usually called the Fertile Crescent. Israel lies on the slender southwestern arm of this curved band. The limited width of the Crescent at this point is caused by the desert pushing the fertile land towards the Mediterranean shores – this can be seen clearly in a modern space photograph of the region – and by the hard tectonic plate in the southeast pressing against the marine geological strata which formed under the sea and which started to fold and rise mainly in the upper cretaceous era, some 120 million years ago. Thus the central mountain ridge of this country was formed, consisting of the remains of myriads of small marine organisms as well as larger fossils. These mountains have a relatively cool climate, and therefore attracted man, later serving some of the main trade routes, whereas the valley of the River Jordan and the Dead Sea in the east – part of the great Syrian-African rift valley – is very hot, and the sparse population there existed chiefly because of the special fruits grown in the region.

In the past, communication between countries took the form of direct physical contact between their populations, be it for commercial, cultural or martial aims. The geographical conditions of the Holy Land channelled the flow of traders and armies through the narrow strip of land between the River Jordan and the Mediterranean Sea, and historical events chased each other in proximity of time and space. Here the nations of the region met, alternately building and destroying: cultures were generated, and cities and villages were razed. Three universal values were born in this region: the alphabet, belief in a single God, and the Bible, the Book of Books.

Within the context of the present volume the location of the country as well as its access routes are of interest. In numerous mediaeval maps the Holy Land is depicted as the centre of the world, but this reflects a spiritual, not a geographical-physical, attitude. In the past the country could be approached from the north, east and southwest by land routes only. The Mediterranean Sea served the maritime routes from Europe and North Africa. The Red Sea and the Gulf of Elat served only small populations, and were endangered by pirates and slave traders. Today most visitors and immigrants arrive by air.

A Brief History of a Historical Region

The third millennium B.C.E. already witnessed fortified cities, palaces and temples in the land of Canaan. Ancient Jericho, the ruins of which can be seen at Tell e-Sultan, is much older still. The 19th and 18th centuries, during the Middle Bronze age, were the era of the patriarchs of Israel: Abraham, Isaac, and Jacob and his offspring. They lived a semi-nomadic life not differing much from that of present-day bedouins. From the book of Genesis we know that they pitched their tents at various times near the Canaanite cities of Shechem (later Nablus), Hebron and Bethel, and that they were on friendly terms with such Canaanite kings as Malki-Zedek of Shalem (Jerusalem) and Avimelech of Gerar.

At this time the country was inhabited by, among others, Canaanites, Amorites, Hittites, Hivites, Perizzites, Jebusites and Girgashites. In the 18th century B.C.E. the Hyksos conquered Canaan and held it for some 200 years. During the second half of the 16th, and the 15th and 14th centuries B.C.E., Egypt of the "New Kingdom", under the 18th and 19th dynasties, held the hegemony over Canaan. The annals of the ties – administrative, military and commercial – between Egypt and the Canaanite city-states are recorded on the clay letters of the first half of the 14th century B.C.E. found in the royal archives at Tell el-Amarna on the Middle Nile. Among the places from which these letters were dispatched to Egypt were Jerusalem, Ashqelon, Lakhish, Gezer, Shechem, Megiddo, Ta'anakh, 'Akko and Hazor (the official modern spelling is used here) – all well-known inhabited places today, after the revival of the State of Israel.

The Israelites which went down to Egypt because of a heavy drought perhaps in the 18th or 17th cent. B.C.E. were enslaved by the Pharaohs; they freed themselves apparently in the 13th century. After travelling for 40 years in the desert, led by Moses and Aaron, they returned to Canaan. Under Joshua, the first Judge, they settled on both banks of the River Jordan. Saul, their first king, founded the monarchy in 1020 B.C.E. But after the reign of King David (who was crowned about 1000 B.C.E.) and his son Solomon, the State split into the kingdom of Israel in the northern part of the country, with Samaria (Shomeron) as capital, and Judah in the south. But the site of the temple built by Solomon in Jerusalem has remained the centre of religious aspirations of Jews up to the present day.

In 722 B.C.E. Israel was invaded by the Assyrians, and in 586 the small state of Judah fell to the Babylonians; Jerusalem and its Temple were laid waste and the inhabitants driven into exile. Some 48 years later Cyrus, king of Persia, who had defeated Babylon, permitted the Jews to return to their homeland and rebuild the Temple.

In 332 B.C.E. the powerful Greek empire of Alexander the Great conquered Israel, but after Alexander's death our country found itself between hammer and anvil – between the territories of the Diadoches, heirs to Alexander's kingdom: the Ptolemids who ruled from Egypt, and the Seleucids with their administrative centre in Syria. The Maccabean revolt (167-141 B.C.E.) brought the Hasmonaean dynasty to power, but the conquest of Jerusalem by Pompey subjected the country to Roman influence. King Herod, of Edomite parentage, married Marianne the Hasmonaean and ruled the country under Roman patronage until 4 B.C.E. Herod, the great builder, left behind him many edifices the remains of which can still be seen today. He also rebuilt the Second Temple; the Western or Wailing Wall, visited today by every Jew coming to Israel, is a remnant of the Temple enclosure of Herod's time.

After Herod's death the Romans strengthened their grip on Judah through the procurators. In 66/67 C.E. the great revolt of the Jews against the Romans broke out in Galilee; in the course of its suppression, in 70 C.E., the Temple was burnt. The country became the province of Palaestina Judaea, and Israel lost its independence for nearly 1900 years. The second revolt, led by Bar-Kokhba in 132-135, only led to Jerusalem being razed to the ground; on its remains the pagan city of Aelia Capitolina was built. The period until 324 C.E. is therefore called the Roman era in Palestine, and alternatively the period of the Mishna and the Talmud, because the Jewish people directed its talents and activities into spiritual channels which, eventually, ensured its survival in exile for nearly two millennia.

In about the year 30 C.E. an event occurred in Palestine which had a deep and lasting impact on humanity. Jesus of Nazareth, born in Bethlehem, who preached a new faith based largely on Judaism, was crucified in Jerusalem. His disciples spread the new religion which was finally adopted even by the Byzantine emperors, who in the 4th century instituted it as State religion in their domains.

The Byzantine empire, heir to Rome in the East, gave its name to the period until 640. During this time most of the ancient synagogues were built in Israel, as well as the majority of mosaic floors which are so typical of Byzantine art and culture. Capernaum, Bar'am, Korazim, Bet-Alfa, Na'aran and Eshtemo'a are but a small number of sites. Many fine churches, too, were erected during this time, in particular the Church of the Nativity in Bethlehem and the Church of the Holy Sepulchre in Jerusalem.

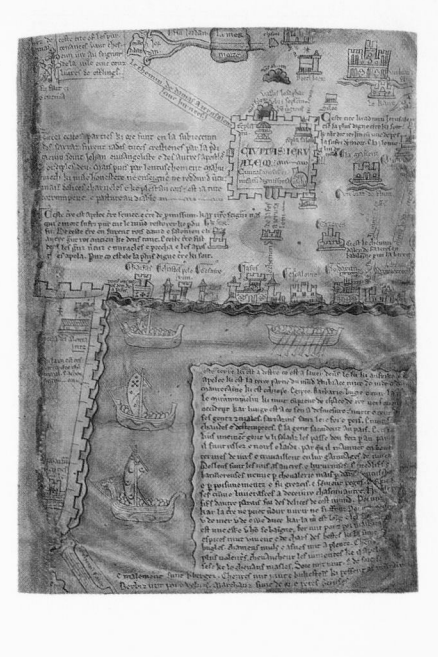

The Moslem Arabs invaded the country in the thirties of the 7th century, and constructed some splendid mosques and other edifices. In 691 the Dome of the Rock was built on the Temple Mount in Jerusalem, and near it the mosque of Aqsa; both stand there to the present day. Ramleh (today Ramla) was the only town in Palestine founded by the Arabs; Jerusalem, where Mohammed ascended to heaven, comes third in religious importance after Mecca and Medina. The Arabs never regarded Palestine as an autonomous geographical or political entity.

Moslem rule was interrupted for two centuries when the crusaders arrived from Europe with the aim of saving the Holy Places from the infidels. In 1099 they took Jerusalem after massacring most of the Moslem and Jewish population. However, in spite of their numerous strongholds and fortresses such as as-Subeiba (Mezudat Nimrod), Montfort, Chateau du Roi at Mi'ilya, Belvoir (at Kokhav haYarden), Chateau Pelerin ('Atlit), Gibelin (Bet Guvrin) and others, their rule did not last; within less than 100 years Saracen pressure reduced Crusader territories to half their original extent. After the battle at the Horns of Hattin near Tiberias and the Moslem conquest of Jerusalem in 1187, the centre of gravity of Crusader activities and administration shifted to Acre (the biblical and today's 'Akko). In 1291 the Latin Kingdom of Jerusalem was finally ousted by the Mamluks. In their turn, the Mamluks ruled Palestine from Egypt for some 220 years – until they too were defeated by the Ottoman Turks. The Mamluks tore down many Crusader strongholds for fear of a renewed crusade, and built numerous religious colleges.

In 1516 the Turks, under Selim I, conquered the country. The Turkish period, characterized by stability – excepting some turbulent interludes – but also by nearly unprecedented neglect, lasted exactly 400 years. However, this was also a time of Jewish immigration and consolidation, albeit of limited extent. In 1917/18 the Holy Land was taken by the Allies during the course of the first World War.

While the Turks still ruled Palestine Theodor Herzl, the founder of Zionism (the secular movement advocating a Jewish return to Zion, Jerusalem), approached the Turkish Sultan and his latter-day ally, the German Kaiser, with the proposal – which was not acted upon – to found a Jewish state in Palestine. However, first real steps in this direction, in the form of the so-called Balfour Declaration, were undertaken by Britain, to which Palestine was entrusted by the League of Nations as a mandated territory following WWI. On 14 May 1948, after a United Nations vote on 29 November 1947 to divide the country into independent Jewish and Arab states, the State of Israel was proclaimed, and opened its gates to Jews from all over the world.

Travels and Pilgrimages to the Holy Land

It can be asserted quite safely that tourism was born in Israel. The Biblical precept "three times in a year shall all thy males appear before the Lord thy God in the place which he shall choose" (Deut. 16, 16) gave rise to internal tourism. Pilgrimages from abroad began after the people of Israel went into exile in the wake of the destruction of the Second Temple, but in particular since the 4th century, when many of the Christian Holy Places were "rediscovered" by Queen Helena of Byzantium, mother of Constantine the Great. However, travel to this country began much earlier.

When the Patriarch Abraham was ordered by the Lord early in the 2nd millennium B.C.E. to leave Mesopotamia and live in the land of Canaan, which was promised to him and his offspring, he started the first journey to that country documented by the Biblical scribe (Gen. 12). After some 60 years Abraham told his servant Eliezer to return to Mesopotamia and bring a wife for his son Isaac from among his family relations. His grandson Jacob-Israel and the latter's sons integrated well in Canaan until, after some 200 years, a famine drove them to Egypt, where they "multiplied greatly" and remained for roughly 400 years. Under Moses and Aaron they left Egypt in an exodus through Sinai and Transjordan which took 40 years to reach Canaan. Within this major mass-movement a shorter journey is described in the Pentateuch, when Moses sent 12 spies to tour the Promised Land. The oversized bunch of grapes which they brought back is today the emblem of the Israeli Government Tourist Office.

About the year 950 B.C.E. King Solomon built the Temple in Jerusalem, thus turning the city into a centre for pilgrims and tourists, at first only from Judah and Israel and later from all over the world.

Two major types of pilgrimages developed in the first centuries after the destruction of the Second Temple, unrelated except for their general goal; they will thus be treated separately. The first comprised the visits to the Holy Land by Jews from the Diaspora, some of whom came only in order to do pilgrimage, while others arrived with the intention to live – and die – in the land of their fathers. The second movement was that of the Christian pilgrims, most of whom came for a visit of several days, weeks or even months to the Holy Places, subsequently returning to their home countries. An exception were the Crusades, which moved masses of people from Europe to the Holy Land.

Since no original documents survive, describing voyages of Jews to this country before the 12th century, Christian pilgrimages – of which much earlier original texts remain, often accompanied by illustrative material, including maps – will be treated first. With the spreading of Christianity in Palestine and its surrounding area as well as in Europe, many Christians wished to visit the places where Jesus Christ had lived and died. The identity of many of these places had been forgotten, but was re-established (though not reliably) by Queen Helena who toured the country in the fourth century. It is interesting to note that some women stand out among the early pilgrims. After Queen Helena we find among others the name – and travel impressions – of Aetheria (Silvia) of Aquitania who toured the Holy Land in about 385. Empress Eudocia, too, wrote down what she saw when visiting for the first time in 439.

The first book describing a tour through the Holy Land was the Itinerarium Burdigalensis, written by an anonymous French traveller apparently before the year 333. It is, however, doubtful whether he actually visited this country, since most of the information seems to have been copied from Jewish sources. Of much greater interest is the "travelogue" written by Arculf, a French bishop who visited Palestine about the year 670. He dictated his impressions to Adamnanus, abbot of the island Iona off the Scottish coast.

The Crusades, between the end of the 11th and the 13th centuries, constitute an important chapter in the annals of travel to the Holy Land. This was the only time when Christians came *en masse* to settle in Palestine. However, they did not take root and were soon pushed back to the sea by the Moslems, partly due to internal strife among the Christians. But some special maps for pilgrims resulted, such as those of Matthew Paris of St. Albans, England, ca. 1250.

The 14th century witnessed a surge of visits by pilgrims, who had not only to obtain permission of the Moslem Mamluk authorities, but, if they were clergymen, they required permission from the Holy See. Thus we find Wilhelm von Bondenselle who chiefly described Jerusalem in 1335, and Sir John Mandeville who visited in the following year leaving behind him a detailed description (not always original) of Palestine. In the following centuries the flow of pilgrims increased.

Many visitors kept a diary and documented their impressions and observations while travelling; others wrote them down after returning home. In some cases the itinerary was written by a person other than the traveller himself. Not only the Holy Places are described; a wealth of information – verbal and graphic – is found in these travel accounts, concerning the physical geography, the flora and fauna as well as the population with its various religions and sects, their habits and dress and even their language and script. In this brief account only selected travellers will be mentioned from among those who left behind important written or graphic evidence of their visits.

Pilgrims arrived as individuals or in small or large groups. Bonifacio de Aragosa came with 60 companions; Bernhard von Breydenbach in 1483 headed a group of 150. Catholics of all denominations and orders headed the list; in the 16th century Protestants joined the flow of pilgrims. All walks of life and all professions were represented. Apart from clergymen, nobles and knights as well as merchants, artisans but also physicians, natural scientists and even artists came and put down on vellum or paper their verbal or graphic impressions. Among the latter were the works of Erhard Reuwich of Utrecht who drew the maps for Bernhard von Breydenbach in 1483, or Cornelis de Bruyn from the Hague (1680) whose fine drawings and paintings embellish many a museum and library today.

Where did these pilgrimages originate? Nearly all European countries were represented, and we shall name but a few travellers from countries not yet mentioned, again only from among those who wrote down their travel impressions. From Germany – Peter Fassbender (1492); Portugal dispatched Pantaleao de Aveiro in 1560; Italy – Leonardi Frescobaldi from Florence (1384); Switzerland – Felix Fabri (1480 and 1483), who wrote the most important travel description in the 15th century; Belgium – Jean Zvallaert or Schwallerten (1586). In central and eastern Europe we meet Nicolai Christoph Radziwill from Poland in 1583; Ulrich Prefat from Slovenia (1546); Martin Kabatnik from Bohemia (1481). Sweden was represented i.a. by Frederick Hasselquist, a disciple of the famous botanist Karl von Linnaeus (1751). Some came anonymously, mentioning only their country, such as the "Spanish Franciscan" in 1555.

And so the flow of the pilgrims increased through the 18th into the 19th cent., when many important geographical investigations and surveys were conducted, some resulting in new and more exact maps. From America too voyagers began to arrive in the last century.

Let us now turn to the travels of Jewish pilgrims, which never ceased since the destruction of the Temple. In 135 C.E., at the end of Bar-Kochba's three-year revolt, the Romans defeated the Jews, who were dispersed all over the world – but they did not defeat Judaism. Every Jew aspired to visit the land of his fathers at least once in his lifetime – Islam later adopted the same attitude towards Mecca – and expressed this in its prayers. But only few of those living in the Diaspora could realize the dream, be it because of economic straits or political, military or religious restrictions. Every Jew who was fortunate enough to make the pilgrimage therefore regarded himself as the representative of his entire congregation, which often supported him financially. This was also the reason for many of the descriptions written by the travellers, who wished to share their religious as well as geographical experiences with their brethren.

The reverse was also true. The ties of the small Jewish community in Palestine with Jews in the Diaspora were hardly ever interrupted. These ties often expressed economic dependence on the part of the small local community. But the Jews in Palestine saw themselves as representing the entire Jewish people in the Holy Land, and particularly at the Holy Places. Much of their income depended on the pilgrims and so, when the flow of the latter was limited or even stopped by local rulers, they suffered economically.

What made a Jew resolve to set out for the Land of Israel, besides general religious fervour? Often it was a vow made in distress. But not always was it possible to make the pilgrimage without delay: sometimes months, and even years, elapsed before a ship was found, or a war or an epidemic had ended. Moreover, a pilgrimage demanded thorough preparations, physical and psychological: in most cases the traveller left his wife and family behind. Practical difficulties, too, were numerous. Some of the writers described for the benefit of their readers the various problems and difficulties to be overcome, e.g. which authorities had to be placated by money, or even where to buy suitable clothing cheaply.

Among the travellers were some who set out prompted by a desire for knowledge; today we would describe them as geographers, ethnographers or historians. These frequently used not the most direct route to Palestine but investigated many distant lands on their devious route to or from the Holy Land. Travelling was dangerous; apart from illness and natural disasters on land and, especially, at sea, wars threatened, as did robbers and pirates. Local rulers demanded tolls, and the impecunious traveller was thrown into jail for ransom. Still, pilgrims continued to brave all hardships.

Jews, too, made the journey mostly singly or in small groups. There were, however, some large groups such as the 1500 who travelled with Rabbi Judah the Hassid between 1700 and 1706; of these, some 500 died on the way. Besides individuals and groups, entire or almost complete communities emigrated to the Land of Israel. Thus, most of the Jews from Yemen in southern Arabia came to Palestine in 1881/82; nearly all the others immigrated after the State of Israel was established in 1948.

Jews came from all countries of the Diaspora – from Babylon and India in the east, from Arabia in the south, from Egypt and North Africa in the west and from Europe in the northwest. What routes did they take? From the numerous descriptions which have survived we can reconstruct the more important ones. Travellers from Spain usually sailed along the North African coast to Egypt, and thence went overland via northern Sinai to Palestine. Italian Jews chiefly sailed in Venetian vessels; a 15th century papal prohibition to carry Jews in ships temporarily led to an increase in overland travellers through Turkey. Pilgrims and travellers from Central Europe mostly reached Venice or Constantinople by land, and thence took to the sea. And finally, all routes from Eastern Europe led to and through Constantinople. From this metropolis again two routes to Jerusalem were favoured – overland, through Ankara, Damascus and Zefat, or by sea, via Rhodes. The main port of disembarkation in Palestine was 'Akko, which had a sizeable Jewish community. Haifa began to function as a port in the 18th century. Only those pilgrims who were in a hurry to reach the Holy City disembarked at Jaffa, where the Jewish community was revived only in about 1830.

Who were the Jewish travellers? As stated above, no original writings from before the 12th century have survived. The renowned Maimonides (or Rambam, Rabbi Moshe ben Maimon), foremost Jewish savant in the Middle Ages, arrived in Jerusalem in 1165 and later left for Egypt where he spent the rest of his days as a court physician. The first detailed Hebrew travel description was composed by Rabbi Benjamin from Tudela in northern Spain around 1170. Among the important visitors in the 13th century were R. Yehuda Alharizi in 1218 and R. Moses ben Nachman, the Ramban, in 1267. Eshtori HaParchi arrived from Spain and Egypt in 1322; he settled in Bet She'an and wrote the first systematic geography of the Holy Land, "Kaftor VaFerach". In the 15th century. came Meshulam

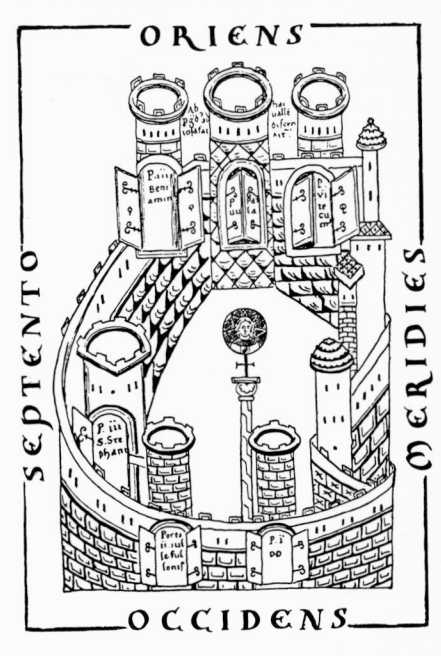

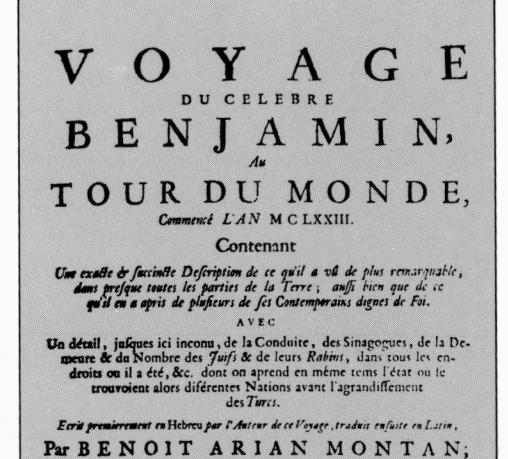

ben Menachem from Volterra in Italy, who noted detailed travel distances in his diary, and in 1473 the anonymous "Traveller from Kandia" (in Crete). Rabbi Moses Basola of Pesaro in Italy visited Palestine in 1521, returned to Italy, and re-immigrated finally, to die in Zefat at the age of 80. Rabbi Yihya el Dhahri from San'a in Yemen, who visited here in 1567 during the course of a worldwide trip, left behind him an interesting book of travel descriptions and moralistic observations in rhyme written in a Yemenite jail. Rabbi Moshe Hirsch, a Torah-scribe from Prague, in 1670 described in detail the various possible travel routes to Palestine.

While there were women among the Jewish travellers, mostly among those who emigrated to Palestine, there was at least one recorded case of a wife who cut short her husband's voyage: in 1764 R. Yehuda of Zalozce was threatened with divorce unless he returned immediately to Poland. Rabbi Nachman of Bratslav, grandson of the Ba'al Shem Tov, founder of Hassidism, visited Jerusalem at the time of Napoleon's Egyptian campaign in order to strengthen Hassidism and to see the Holy Places which his famous grandfather had been unable to visit.

One of the most important visitors was Sir Moses Montefiore, a native of Livorno, Italy, who attained noble rank in England. He visited Palestine seven times (first in 1827, during the Turko-Greek war). On his second visit (1838) he brought with him a plan for lightening the economic burden of the Old Yishuv, the Jewish community in Palestine. His wife Judith kept his travel diary.

Theodor Herzl, the founder of Zionism, planned his visit to Palestine to coincide with that of the German Emperor Wilhelm II in October-November of 1898; Herzl wanted to enlist the latter's help in his endeavours to obtain the consent of the Turkish Sultan to his plan for establishing a Jewish state in Palestine. Herzl was received by the Sultan in Constantinople and by the Kaiser on the Mount of Olives in Jerusalem, but in the end assistance towards founding a National Home for Jews in Plaestine was given by Britain. However, the English curtailed Jewish immigration to Palestine, and only after the State of Israel was established were all Jews permitted free entry into the Holy Land. Jews visiting Israel from all over the world today constitute the majority of tourists to the Holy Land.

The Cartographic Record

Much of our information about the physical geography as well as the settlements and population of the Holy Land is gained from maps. Since a large proportion of the illustrations in this book are indeed reproductions of ancient and old maps, we shall now devote some space to describing the history of cartography of this country. However, we shall deviate from the order in which these maps appear in the book: there they are shown in the order of the subjects they illustrate, while here we shall describe the mapmaker's art in chronological sequence.

While Israel cannot boast of the oldest maps in existence – these originate in Mesopotamia – it certainly can display the longest unbroken continuity of mapping. This results mainly from the country being holy to three major religions, but especially to Christians: the majority of mapmakers during the critical formative stages of cartography in the Middle Ages and early modern times in Europe were Christians. For these it was the Land of Jesus, of Bethlehem, Nazareth and the Sea of Genesareth, and they endeavoured to depict it with all possible detail, as well as the routes leading to it, for the benefit of the pilgrims. Jews, insofar as they produced maps, chiefly depicted the Land of Israel proper, and such Hebrew maps and map-related illustrations were appended to texts explaining the background of biblical events or of the commandments relating to the country itself. Contrary to "Christian" maps they were not appended to Bibles. The Moslems, for whom Palestine was a distant corner of Syria, e-Sham, described it graphically mainly within the framework of larger geographical units.

The oldest original map in existence portraying the Holy Land is the so-called Madaba Map. This was found in the late 19th century as a mosaic floor of a Byzantine church in the small town of Madaba in Jordan, east of the northern end of the Dead Sea. The places shown as well as the Greek inscriptions, reveal that the map was made some time after the middle of the 6th century (according to Avi-Yonah, around 560-565 C.E.). But since its very detailed content depicts Palestine in biblical times, it should be regarded as a historical map, and not only as an ancient one. It was constructed by an unknown artist from about $2^{1}/_{2}$ million tesserae or small stone cubes of suitable colours. Since all places shown lie on one or the other of the paved Roman roads in Palestine, it may have been based on an older road map, perhaps of Roman origin. It may, however, be safely assumed that its creator made

17

use of the Onomastikon, a gazetteer of 983 biblical place names compiled by Eusebius, bishop of Caesarea, in the 4th century. Like most ancient maps the Madaba map was truly "oriented", i.e. it showed east at the top. The display of Jerusalem in this map is most revealing, showing 43 identifiable public buildings, many of them churches. It can thus be regarded as the oldest detailed urban map in existence.

Few are the maps originating in the Middle Ages. The literate stratum of the European population was chiefly composed of the clergy, and in particular monks. The mediaeval church, engaged in consolidating its position and, like all religions, being founded on belief and not on information, stifled most secular research and pursuit of knowledge. This applied to geography too, and as a result only few maps representing geographical reality were produced. On the other hand, there developed in the later mediaeval era a new type of stylized "map" depicting the world as a flat circular disk surrounded by the "mare oceanum". The three known continents were shown schematically within the circle, with Asia at the top, Europe in the lower left and Africa in the lower right sector. They were divided by the main water bodies drawn in the form of a letter T. The vertical stroke represented the Mediterranean Sea, and the horizontal one – the River Don (Tanais), the Black and Aegean Seas and, to the right, the River Nile. These maps, differing in detail, were thus popularly called O-T or Orbis Terrarum maps; they were oriented to the east, and many had Jerusalem at the centre. The tradition of showing the Holy City of Jerusalem, or at least the Holy Land (and sometimes Paradise) at the hub of the world persisted in some quarters until the 16th century, as witness Heinrich Bünting's map of the world of 1588 in the shape of a clover leaf: the center of the trifolium represents Jerusalem.

Another interesting – and beautiful – example of a circular mappa mundi (i.e. world map) with Jerusalem at its centre is the so-called Ebstorf map. This is already much more elaborate (though most of the detail is fictitious or at least geographically erroneous). Perhaps in order to qualify for Church display (it served as an altarpiece in the German village of Ebstorf), Christ's head, outspread hands and feet were added to the circular body of the map.

Some time after bursting out of the Arabian peninsula to the northeast, north and northwest in the 7th and 8th century, the Moslems too began to make maps. In the "Islamic Atlas" – which was not one particular atlas but a fixed framework of 21 maps, mostly dating from the 10th and 11th centuries – Palestine appears as a small part of the Mediterranean Sea coast. This sea was depicted schematically in the form of a bottle, a vial or a water-skin, probably in order to facilitate orientation and determining prayer direction towards Mecca. These maps show the four cardinal directions in their four corners; thus, with janūb, south, in the upper left corner, they pointed towards southwest, and not southward as is often assumed. But later Moslem maps such as those by Idrisi (of ca. 1150) are indeed directed to the south.

One of the most intriguing, interesting and innovative maps ever found is the Peutinger Map (Tabula Peutingeriana). Drawn probably in the 12th or 13th century, this was acquired by the town clerk of Augsburg in southern Germany, Conrad Peutinger, in 1507. It has the form of a very elongated vellum scroll and shows the Roman empire from Gaul in the west to India in the east. It is one of the earliest examples of a thematic map, since it represents in detail the huge network of paved Roman roads and road stations, even indicating the distances between the latter, with a total of some 70,000 Roman miles or about 100,000 kilometers! This is, indeed, a true travel map. Furthermore, cities, towns and villages as well as temples and shrines of differing size and importance are represented by class symbols, and this, too, was an innovation. The map was cut into 12 segments (the first, westernmost one, was lost), with Palestine and its Roman roads shown on the sixth segment. The elongated form was achieved by narrowing down sea areas to thin wavy bands of greyish green. Since this was done with the specific purpose of reducing its width to fit into a scroll suitable for travel, the Peutinger Table should on no account be simply labelled incorrect. Drawn in the late Middle Ages, it is apparently a copy of a much older map drawn some 800 or 900 years previously, showing the road net of the Roman-Byzantine empire around the year 365.

The Crusades left a distinctive mark on the cartography of the Holy Land, with many maps of the two capital cities, Jerusalem and 'Akko (St. Jean d'Acre) stemming from that time. But maps showing the pilgrim route from Europe to the Holy City were also produced, such as that by the English monk Matthew Paris in about 1250. Drawn some 60 years after the battle of Hattin, his map of Palestine shows Akko 13 times larger in area than Jerusalem. The Crusader city maps of Jerusalem are mostly schematic in form and show a cross-like framework of streets within circular city walls, and thus they resemble the circular O-T world maps. However, besides these, no doubt drawn by persons who had never visited Jerusalem, some excellent city maps of almost "modern" precision have survived from that time.

In 1321 the Venetian nobleman Marino Sanudo presented Pope John XXII with a proposal to retake the Holy Places from the infidels. To his "Liber Secretorum Fidelium Crucis" (Book of Secrets for Crusaders) were appended

TABVLA
ITINERARIA
ex illustri
PEUTINGERORUM
BIBLIOTHECA
Quæ Augustæ Vindelicorum
Beneficio
MARCI VELSERI
Septem-viri Augustani
In Lucem
edita.

several maps by Pietro Vesconte, among them the first detailed map of the Holy Land in which its true shape can be recognized, though still oriented to the east. In its later printed form it even contained a reference grid of squares, like modern topographic maps.

Perhaps no pre-18th century pilgrimage resulted in such detailed and extensive verbal and graphic descriptions as that by Bernhard von Breydenbach in 1483. The Flemish painter Erhard Reuwich who accompanied the German deacon from Mainz portrayed not only the important stations of the pilgrimage (inter alia Venice, Corfu and Rhodes), but especially Palestine. His map of the Holy Land is of special interest: though oriented to the east, it incorporates a highly detailed view of Jerusalem of nearly photographical precision, directed westward – the direction in which the Holy City is seen at its best, from the Mount of Olives!

Far-reaching developments in cartography took place when, during the Renaissance, the geographical and cartographic works of Claudios Ptolemaios (Ptolemy), 2nd century geographer and astronomer in Alexandria, were translated into Latin after having been forgotten in Europe for over a thousand years. Ptolemy's original maps had been lost, but now, in the 14th and 15th centuries, they were reconstructed with the aid of the text and list of places found in his great 8-part work, Geographiki Yphigesis, i.e. Instructions for drawing the Earth. In the late 15th and 16th century editions of this work some "tabulae modernae", modern maps, were added to the 27 "original" Ptolemaian maps – among these a map of the Holy Land based on that of Pietro Vesconte. Whereas the latter was oriented to the east, the former were directed northward. Nearly two centuries elapsed before the latter direction was adopted almost universally.

New maps of Palestine now began to appear at brief intervals. The majority were labelled "Terra Sancta" and thus were "historical" maps depicting the Holy Land in biblical times (usually showing the lots of the tribes of Israel) or even earlier. Some maps even depict the "four cities of the plain" Sodom, Gomorrah, Admah and Zeboim, before their destruction by fire and sulphur – and omit the Dead Sea. Many maps show the route of the exodus from Egypt. But some earlier travels are also represented: Abraham Ortelius, a 16th century. Flemish cartographer, published a map showing the travels of the Patriarch Abraham from Mesopotamia to Canaan. The voyages of the Apostles were also shown in maps.

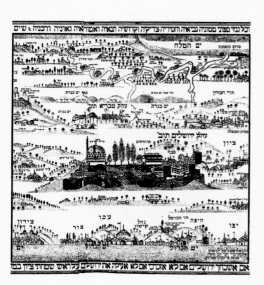

The introduction of letterpress printing by Johannes Gutenberg in the 15th century led to a drastic proliferation of maps. One of the first two printed maps (in a book printed in Lübeck in 1475) showed the Holy Land; the other was a world map centered on Jerusalem. Printing in those times was in monochrome; colouring was sometimes added by hand.

Mention should also be made of maps by Jewish cartographers. These are not very numerous, and in some cases the maps were copied from Christian map-makers (who often copied from each other). This is also true of the oldest printed map in Hebrew extant today, which was copied (and embellished) in 1621 by Jacobo Justus (Ya'akov Hazaddik) in Amsterdam from Christian Adrichom's map of 1590. Even as late as 1836 a map by Rabbi Aaron ben Moshe of Grodno perpetuated, in a Hebrew map, a geographical error introduced by Christian cartographers, namely the River Kishon joining the Mediterranean with the Sea of Galilee.

There were, however, exceptions. In ca. 1375 Abraham Cresques, a Jewish "Magister mappamundorum et bruxellarum", i.e. master of world maps and compasses, from Maiorca, produced the excellent so-called Catalan Atlas, beautifully executed, which also included the Holy Land.

Returning now to modern times, we find that the first map of our country based on compass traverses was produced, under the direction of Pierre Jacotin, by the French expeditionary army which conquered Egypt in 1798 and, in 1799, proceeded to Palestine, reaching 'Akko before being defeated by the Turks and the British. The introduction, shortly before, of the metre as standard unit of measure led to the "modern" map scale of 1:100,000.

The first topographic map of the country, at a scale of one inch to the mile (1:63,360) was prepared by a surveying team sent out by the London-based Palestine Exploration Fund between 1870 and 1877, and published in 1880. This excellent map in 26 sheets served not only Bible scholars but also the British army in Palestine during the early stages of World War I. Its reduction, at the turn of the century, to a scale of 1:253,440 (1/4 inch to the mile) resulted in the first popular multipurpose map of the country; later Jewish mapmakers such as Haim Arlosoroff, Ze'ev Jabotinski and A. J. Brawer based their maps on it. It can be assumed that Theodor Herzl, too, consulted it or one of its derivatives while writing "The Jewish State" and "Altneuland".

Jerusalem, 1987

c. 1900 B.C.E.

And God said...

Frontispiece of the "Schocken Bible", Genesis (enlarged),
with 46 illustrations of Biblical tales. Manuscript, thirteenth century.

Abraham

Originally called Abram, his name was changed by the Lord to Abraham to signify that he would become "Father of many nations". He was the first and foremost founding father of the Israelites. The major part of his life is recounted in Chapters 11-25 of the Book of Genesis. Abraham was the founder of the monotheistic belief. At the Lord's command he left Haran accompanied by his wife, and came to the Land of Canaan.

In Jewish tradition Abraham more than any other figure, symbolizes the staunch faith which enables Man to accept all of God's decrees with love. He also stands for love of one's fellow-man, and generous hospitality.

He fought against Chedorlaomer, King of Elam, who took his son-in-law Lot prisoner. When he returned from the war he was blessed by Melchizedek, King of Salem, priest of the most high God: "Blessed be Abraham of the most high God, possessor of heaven and earth."

At the age of one hundred and twenty seven, his wife Sarah passed away and was buried in the cave of Machpelah purchased by Abraham for that purpose from Efron the Hittite.

Abraham lived to be one hundred and seventy-five and he, too, was buried alongside his wife in Hebron.

Opening page of the first printed Hebrew Bible. Printed in Soncino at the end of the fifteenth century.

"...Now the Lord had said unto Abram: Get thee out of thy country, and from thy kindred, and from thy father's house, unto a land that I will shew thee. And I will make of thee a great nation, and I will bless thee and make thy name great; and thou shalt be a blessing."

(Genesis 12:1-2)

Abraham and Sarah leaving the city of Ur on their journey to the Land of Canaan. From a fourteenth century French manuscript.

So Abram departed, as the Lord had spoken unto him; and Lot went with him: and Abram was seventy and five years old when he departed out of Haran. And Abram took Sara his wife, and Lot his brother's son, and all their substance that they had gathered, and the souls that they had gotten in Haran; and they went forth to go into the land of Canaan; and into the land of Canaan they came. And Abram passed through the land unto the place of Sichem, unto the plain of Moreh. And the Canaanite was then in the land.

And the Lord appeared unto Abram, and said, Unto thy seed will I give this land: and there builded he an altar unto the Lord, who appeared unto him.

And he removed from thence unto a mountain on the east of Beth-el, and pitched his tent, having Beth-el on the west, and Hai on the east: and there he builded an altar unto the Lord, and called upon the name of the Lord. And Abram journeyed, going on still toward the south. And Abram went up out of Egypt, he, and his wife, and all that he had, and Lot with him, into the south. And Abram was very rich in cattle, in silver, and in gold. And he went on his journeys from the south even to Beth-el, unto the place where his tent had been at the beginning, between Beth-el and Hai; Unto the place of the altar, which he had made there at the first; and there Abram called on the name of the Lord.

And the Lord said unto Abram, after that Lot was separated from him, Lift up now thine eyes, and look from the place where thou art northward, and southward, and eastward, and westward: For all the land which thou seest to thee will I give it, and to thy seed for ever. And I will make thy seed as the dust of the earth; so that if a man can number the dust of the earth, then shall thy seed also be numbered. Arise, walk through the land in the length of it and in the breadth of it: for I will give it unto thee.

Then Abram removed his tent, and came and dwelt in the plain of Mamre, which is in Hebron, and built there an altar unto the Lord."

(Genesis 12:4-9; 13:1-4, 14-18)

XXII.

Nach diesen geschichten/versuchte Gott Abraham vnd sprach zu jm/Abraham/Vñ er antwortet/hie bin ich/ Vnd er sprach/Nim Isaac deinen einigen son/den du lieb hast/vnd gehe hin jnn das land Moria/vnd opffer jn da selbs zum brand opffer auff einem berge/den ich dir sagen werd/Da stund Abraham des morgens frue auff/vnd gürtet seinen esel/vnd nam mit sich zween Knaben vnd seinen son Isaac/vnd spaltet holtz zum brandopffer/macht sich auff/vnd gieng hin an den ort/dauon jm Gott gesagt hatte.

Am dritten tag hub Abraham seine augen auff/vnd sahe die stet von ferne/vnd sprach zu seinen knaben/Bleibt jr hie mit dem esel/Ich vnd der knabe wollen dort hin gehen / vnd wenn wir angebetet haben/wollen wir widder zu euch komen/Vnd Abraham nam das holtz zum brandopffer/vnd legts auff seinen son Isaac / Er aber nam das fewr vnd messer jnn seine hand/vnd giengen die beide mit einander.

Da sprach Isaac zu seinem vater Abraham / Mein vater / Abraham antwort/Hie bin ich/mein son/Vnd er sprach/Sihe/hie ist feur vnd holtz/wo ist aber das schaf zum brandopffer ? Abraham antwort/Gott wird mir zeigen/ mein son / das schaf zum brandopffer/ vnd giengen die beide mit einander.

Vnd als sie kamen an die stet/die jm Gott saget/bawet Abraham daselbs einen altar/vnd legt das holtz drauff / vnd band seinen son Isaac/legt jn auff den altar oben auff das holtz/vnd recket seine hand aus/vnd fasset das messer/das er seinen son schlachtet.

C   Da rieff

The Sacrifice of Isaac.
From the German Lutheran Bible, 1545.

Abraham

Abraham Ortelius (1527-1598)

Ortelius, originally Abraham Ortel, was born in Antwerp in 1527. He was the disciple of Gerardus Mercator (1512-1594). His work is known to have had a great influence on the geography and cosmology of the modern era. When he finished his studies (Latin, Greek and Mathematics), he became involved in the commercial sale of books, as well as in the sale and production of maps.

Before he produced his great work, the "Theatrum Orbis Terrarum" ("Theater of the Terrestrial Sphere"), he published many maps. In 1554 he published a map of the world in eight parts. This was followed by a map of Egypt in two parts (1554), a map of Asia in two parts (1557), and a map of Spain in six parts (1570).

The Map

Source: "Theatrum Orbis Terrarum" ("Theatre of the Terrestrial Sphere"). Published in English, 1606. Compilation: Tilemann Stolz (Stella). Engraving and publication: Ortelius. Technique: copper engraving. Size of original: 35.5 x 46.2 cm.

The map describes the life and travels of our forefather Abraham. It shows the Land of Canaan before the destruction of Sodom and Gomorrah. A woven carpet hanging on the wall depicts the Land, and twenty-two sketches describe the life of Abraham. In the top left hand corner, a small map describes Abraham's route from Aram Naharayim (Mesopotamia) to Shechem.

The Atlas "Theatrum Orbis Terrarum"

The "Theatrum Orbis Terrarum" by Ortelius was published in 1570. It contains a collection of maps unique in size, format, and to a great degree, in style. This collection is not the first "atlas". It was Mercator who first used that term. Nonetheless, it is undoubtedly the first systematic collection of maps of all the lands of the then-known world. It rested on knowledge accumulated from the time of Ptolemy until the time of Ortelius.

Mercator, who valued the talents and abilities of Ortelius, wrote to him in a letter: "You deserve the highest praise for choosing the best and turning it into a single creation. Even so you gave honour and position to all of the cartographers who took part in your work." Ortelius indeed deserved the title of "Creator of the first modern atlas."

The first collection included 70 maps on 53 pages, among them a world map (signed by Franz Hoghenberg, the engraver), four continental maps and 65 regional maps. In the first edition, 87 cartographers were mentioned. By 1603 that number had reached 183. Ortelius strove to acquire the best maps. He produced copies of the original that were as precise as possible, and he always added the name of the cartographer.

Portrait of Abraham Ortelius

Title page from "The Great Bible"
Translated and presented to King Henry VIII. Parchment, London 1539.

Greek edition, 1516.

Swedish edition, 1618.

Polish edition, 1563.

French edition, 1535.

Italian edition, 1481.

German edition, 1534.

First page of the Book of Genesis

Map of the Holy Land by Tilemann Stella
from the atlas by Abraham Ortelius, 1570 edition.

World map
from the atlas by Abraham Ortelius, 1570 edition.

THEA
TRVM
ORBIS
TERRA
RVM

Title page
from the atlas by Abraham Ortelius, 1570 edition.

c. 950 B.C.E.

Build Me a House

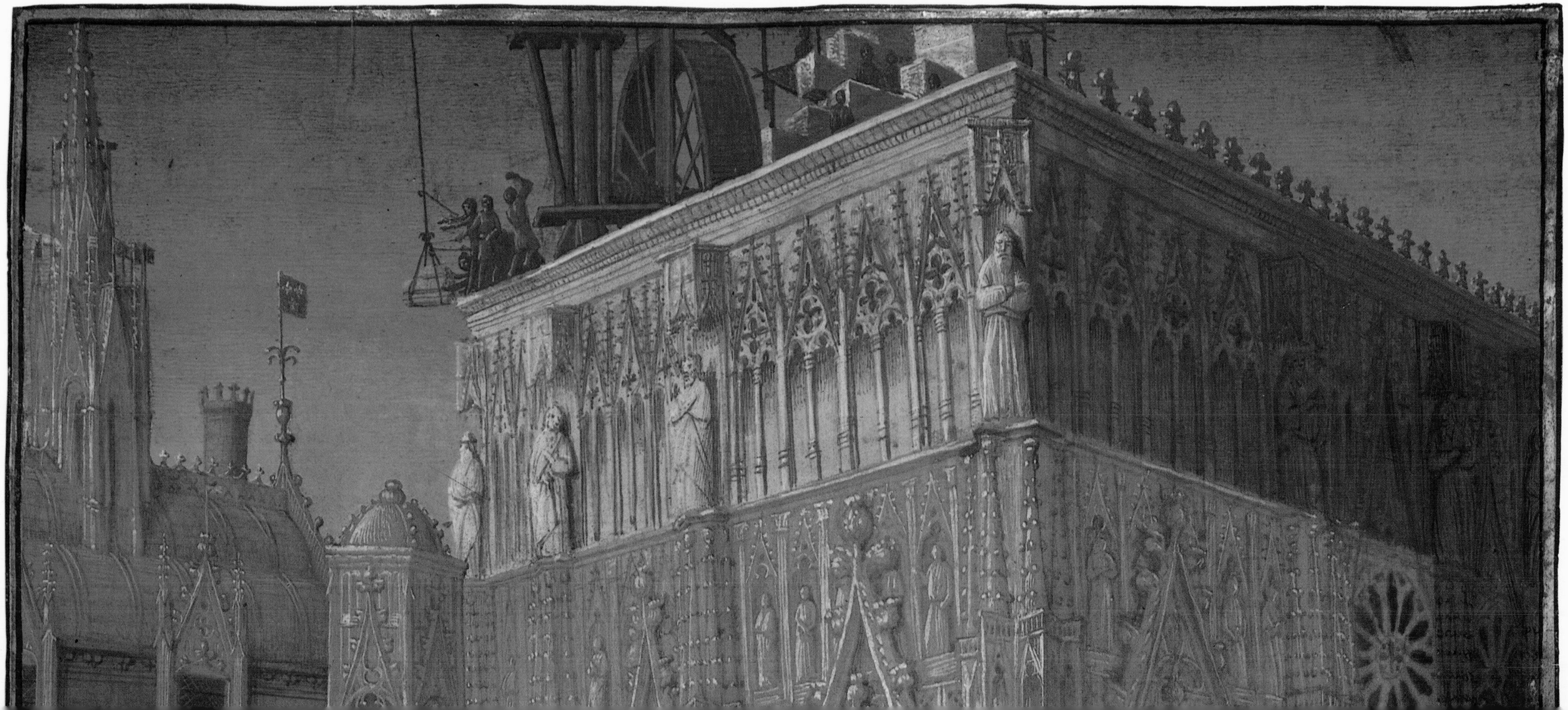

Construction of the Temple by King Solomon,
from "Jewish Antiquities", by Josephus Flavius. Manuscript and illustrations by Jean Fouquet, fifteenth century.

King Solomon

King Solomon (tenth century B.C.E.), son of David, King of Israel and Bathsheba, was anointed for the kingship by the priest Zadok. Solomon apparently ruled at his father David's side for three years (967-965 B.C.E.). From 965 to 928 B.C.E. he ruled alone.

Great public edifices were built during his reign, the most important of these being the Temple, which became a focal centre for pilgrimages.

Although he expanded the boundaries of his kingdom, Solomon managed to maintain cordial relations with his neighbors. King Solomon was regarded as the "wisest among men", and as a wise and fair judge. The Books of Proverbs, Ecclesiastes, and Song of Songs are attributed to him. He ruled over all of Israel and Judea for almost forty years and was buried in Jerusalem.

Candelabrum.
From a fifteenth century Passover Haggadah.

"Even them will I bring to my holy mountain and make them joyful in my house of prayer: their burnt offerings and their sacrifices shall be accepted upon mine altar; for mine house shall be called an house of prayer for all people."

(Isaiah 56:7)

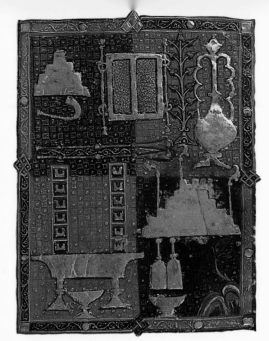

Vessels of the Temple.
From a fifteenth century Passover Haggadah.

Solomon began to build the temple in the fourth year of his reign, in the second month, which the Macedonians call Artemisius, and the Hebrews, Iar, five hundred and ninety-two years after the Exodus out of Egypt; but one thousand and twenty-two years from Abraham's coming out of Mesopotamia, into Canaan, and after the deluge one thousand four hundred and forty years; and from Adam the first man who was created until Solomon built the temple, there had passed in all three thousand one hundred and two years. Now that year on which the temple began to be built, was already the twelfth year of the reign of Hiram; but from the building of Tyre, to the building of the temple, there had passed two hundred and forty years.

Now, therefore, the king laid the foundation of the temple very deep in the ground, and the materials were strong stones, and such as would resist the force of time; these were to unite themselves with the earth, and become a basis for a sure foundation for that edifice which was to be erected: they were to be so strong, in order to sustain with ease those vast superstructures, and precious ornaments, whose own weight was to be not less than the weight of those high and heavy buildings which the king designed to be very ornamental and magnificent.

They erected its entire body quite up to the roof of white stone...

...And as he enclosed the walls with boards of cedar, so he fixed on them plates of gold, which had sculptures upon them: so that the whole temple dazzled the eyes of such as entered, by the splendour of the gold that was on every side. Now the whole structure of the temple was made with great skill, of polished stones, and those laid together so very smoothly and harmoniously, that there appeared to the spectators no sign of any hammer, or other instrument of architecture...

...He also laid the floor of the temple with plates of gold. And he added doors to the gate of the temple agreeable to the measure of the height of the wall, but in breadth twenty cubits; and on them fixed gold plates. And, in a word, he left no part of the temple, neither internal nor external, but what was covered with gold.

Now Solomon sent for an artificer out of Tyre, whose name was Hiram...This man was skillful in all sorts of work; but his chief skill lay in working of gold and silver, and brass; by whom were made all the mechanical works about the temple, according to the will of Solomon.

...When King Solomon had finished these large and beautiful buildings, and had laid up his donations in the temple, and all this in the interval of seven years.

...Nay, moreover this help is what I implore of thee, not for the Hebrews only, when they are in distress; but when any shall come hither from any ends of the world, and shall return from their sins, and implore thy pardon, do thou then pardon them, and hear their prayer. For hereby all shall learn that thou wast pleased with the building of this house".

The Holy of Holies.
From a fourteenth century French manuscript.

King Solomon

(From Josephus Flavius: "Jewish Antiquities", Book II, Part 8, English edition, 1812.)

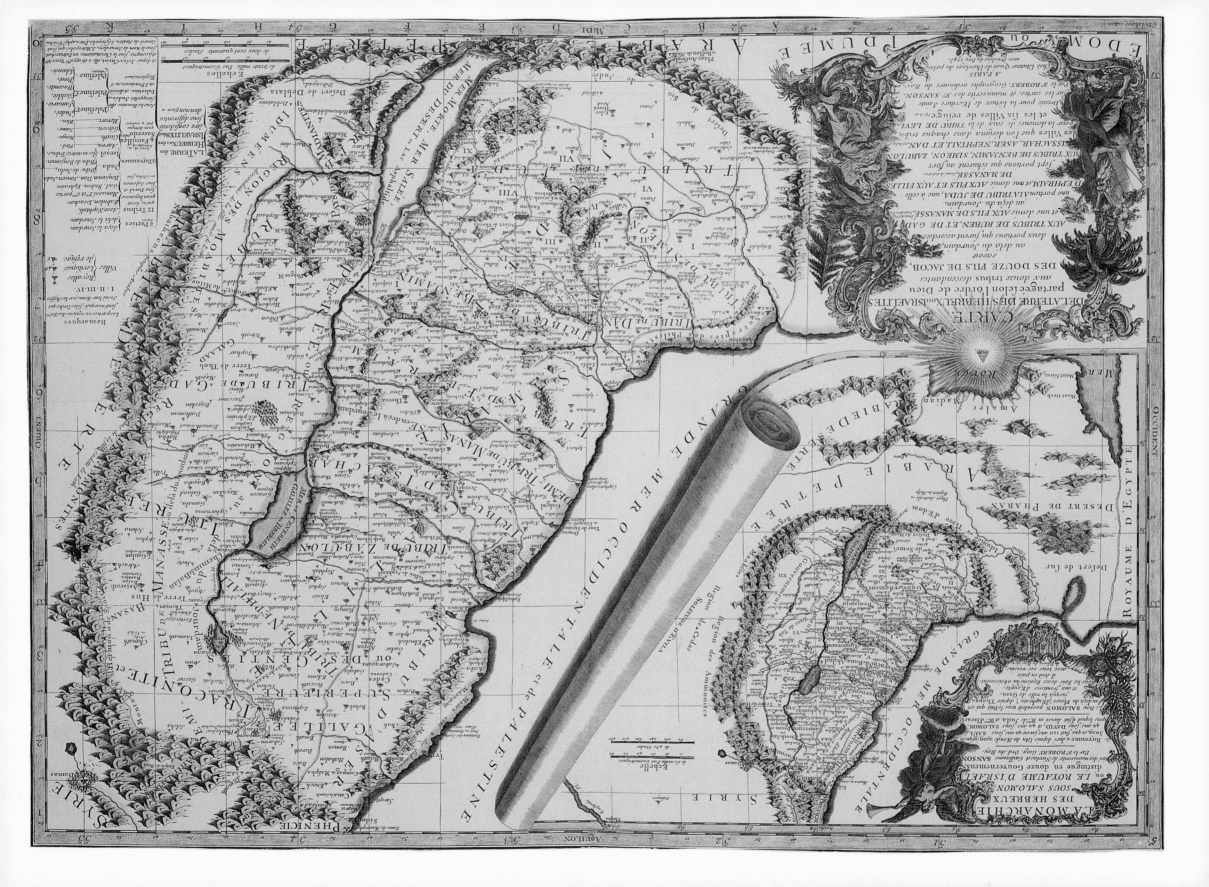

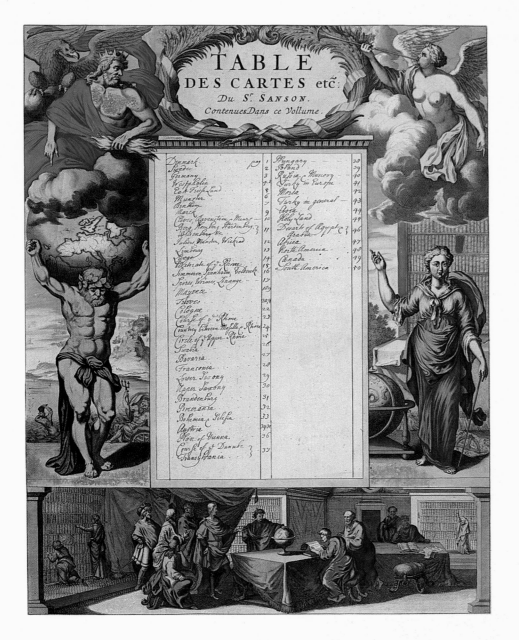

Atlas Title-page
The title-page shows a handwritten list of the maps contained in the atlas, including a map of the Land of Israel. Paris, 1745.

Nicholas Sanson (1600-1667)

Founder of the Geographical and Cartographic school of seventeenth century France. For many years his works were published by members of his family (his sons Adrian and Guillaume, his heir Moullard Sanson Pierre, and his nephew Robert de Vaugondy).

Nicholas Sanson worked together with Pierre Mariette. For a while Mariette was his partner. In his maps, Sanson dispensed with the ornateness that characterized Flemish cartography, and concentrated on content. He published several atlases, the first of which appeared in 1658, as well as maps of all regions of the earth. These served as a foundation for the maps and publications that his family produced after him.

The Map

The map before us is based on previous maps of the Sanson family. It was published by Robert de Vaugondy in the atlas that appeared in 1745. This map depicts the kingdom of Solomon and the division of the Land of Israel into tribal lots. The map in the centre describes the lots of the twelve tribes of Israel and their borders as determined by Joshua. In the second map, found in the upper left corner of the main map, we can see an open scroll showing the borders of the kingdom of Solomon as described in the Scriptures.

In the illustration appearing in the upper left-hand corner of the map, we read the caption: "The Kingdom of the Hebrews under Solomon". There we find depicted the twelve districts of the kingdom. The realms of Saul, David and Solomon are mentioned in the illustration. These kings ruled from 2909 to 3029 after the Creation, a period of about 120 years. After Solomon's rule, the kingdom was divided into the realms of Judea and Israel.

Moreover, the borders of the kingdom of Solomon are described here. Of this the illustration reads, "All the nations in this region lived peacefully with their neighbours."

In the lower portion of the illustration shows a small drawing which depicts the Judgment of Solomon.

LANDMARKS OF THE ERA

King Solomon's Judgment.
From a Passover Haggadah, 1751.

King Solomon receives the Queen of Sheba.
Drawing from a German Bible, 1483.

Title page of the Book of Ecclesiastes.
From a Hebrew manuscript, Germany fifteenth century.

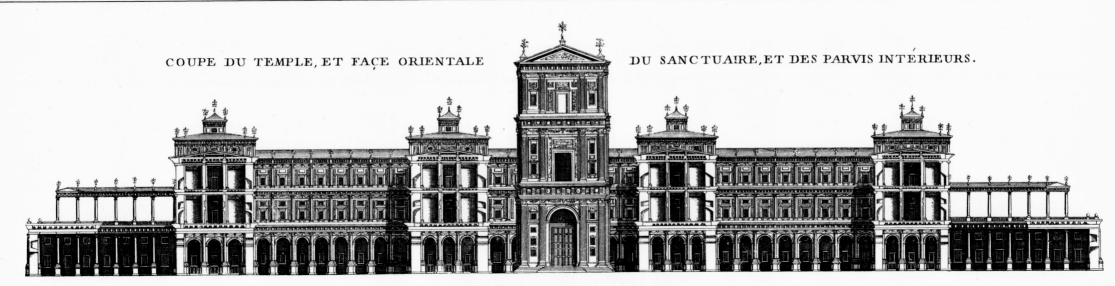

COUPE DU TEMPLE, ET FACE ORIENTALE   DU SANCTUAIRE, ET DES PARVIS INTÉRIEURS.

A section depicting the front of the Temple.
Copper engraving, eighteenth century.

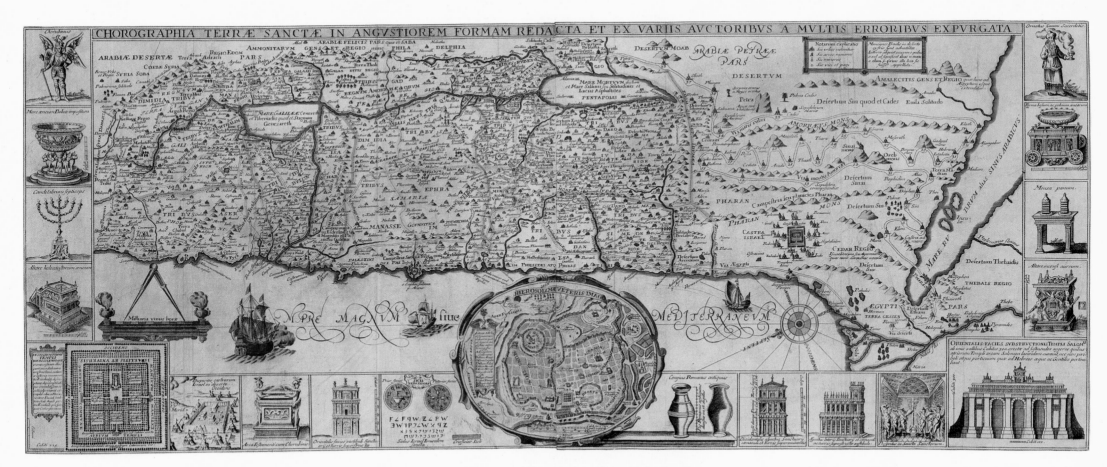

Isaac Tirion (–1769), Map of the Holy Land
with a map of Jerusalem and eighteen depictions of vessels of the Temple. Amsterdam, 1720.

70 C.E.

TRUMPETS
OF
THE LEGIONS

Silver coin of Agrippa I (37-44)
Agrippa's father, Aristobulus, riding in a chariot. Above him, written in Greek: "Coin of King Agrippa". (Enlarged.)

Titus

Titus Flavius Vespasianus (c.39-81 C.E.) was Emperor of Rome. Titus accompanied his father Vespasian, who arrived in the Holy Land in the year 66 in order to suppress the revolt in Galilee. Titus also conquered Yotapata, sparing the life of its commander, Joseph Ben Matityahu (Josephus Flavius). In the year 69, Titus was entrusted with the conquest of Jerusalem, where Jewish rebels who fled the captured towns of Galilee had subsequently gathered. Under his command four legions, reinforced by additional soldiers, surrounded Jerusalem. The siege of the city began during the feast of Passover in the year 70 and after heavy fighting the Temple was set on fire on the 9th of Ab (8 September 70), thereby putting an end to organized anti-Roman resistance in the land of Judea.

Head of Titus on gold coin with legend: Imp (erator) Titus Caes (ar) Vespasianus P(ontifex) M(aximus), year 71.

"...We have certainly had God for our assistant in this war: and it was no other than God who ejected the Jews out of these fortifications. For what could the hands of man, or any machines, do towards overthrowing these towers?"...

(From Josephus Flavius, "The Jewish War", Book VI, Part 9.)

Destruction of the Temple
by the soldiers of Titus
from Jean Fouquet's "Josephus Flavius".
Fifteenth century French manuscript.

Their times also for sleeping, watching, and rising are notified beforehand by the sound of trumpets. Nor is any thing done without such a signal. When they are to go out of their camp, the trumpet gives a sound: at which time no body lies still; but at the first intimation they take down their tents; and all is made ready for their going out. Then do the trumpets sound again, to order them to get ready for the march. Then they lay their baggage suddenly upon their mules, and other beasts of burden; and stand as at the place of starting, ready to march.

They also set fire to their camp: because it will be easy for them to erect another, and that it may not ever be of use to their enemies. Then do the trumpets give a sound the third time that they are to go out; in order to excite those that, on any account, are a little tardy: that so no one may be out of his rank when the army marches. Then the crier stands at the general's right hand, and asked them, thrice, in their own tongue, whether they be ready to go out to war, or not? To which they reply, as often with a loud and cheerful voice, "We are ready." And this they do almost before the question is asked them, as if they were inspired with a kind of martial fury: and at the same time that they so cry out, they lift up their right hands...

Thus was Jerusalem taken, in the second year of the reign of Vespasian, on the eighth day of the month Gorpieus, or Elul. It had been taken five times before: though this was the second time of its desolation. For Shishak, King of Egypt, and after him Antiochus, and after him Pompey, and after them Sosius and Herod, took the city: but still preserved it. But before all these, the King of Babylon conquered it, and made it desolate: one thousand, four hundred, sixty-eight years, and six months, after it was first built. But he who first built it was a potent man among the Canaanites: and is in our own tongue called Melchizedeck, the Righteous King. For such he really was. On which account he was there the first priest of God; and first built the temple there, and called the city Jerusalem: which was formerly called Salem. However, David, king of the Jews, ejected the Canaanites, and settled his own people therein. It was demolished entirely by the Babylonians, four hundred, seventy-seven years, and six months after him. And from king David, who was the first of the Jews who reigned therein, to this destruction under Titus, were one thousand, one hundred, and seventy-nine years. But from its first building till this last destruction were two thousand, one hundred, and seventy-seven years. Yet hath not its great antiquity, nor its vast riches, nor the diffusion of its nation over all the habitable earth; nor the greatness of the veneration paid to it on a religious account, been sufficient to preserve it from being destroyed. And thus ended the siege of Jerusalem."

Titus meeting Josephus Flavius after the siege of Jotapata.
From a fifteenth century French manuscript.

Titus

(From Josephus Flavius: "The Jewish War", Book III , Part 5.)

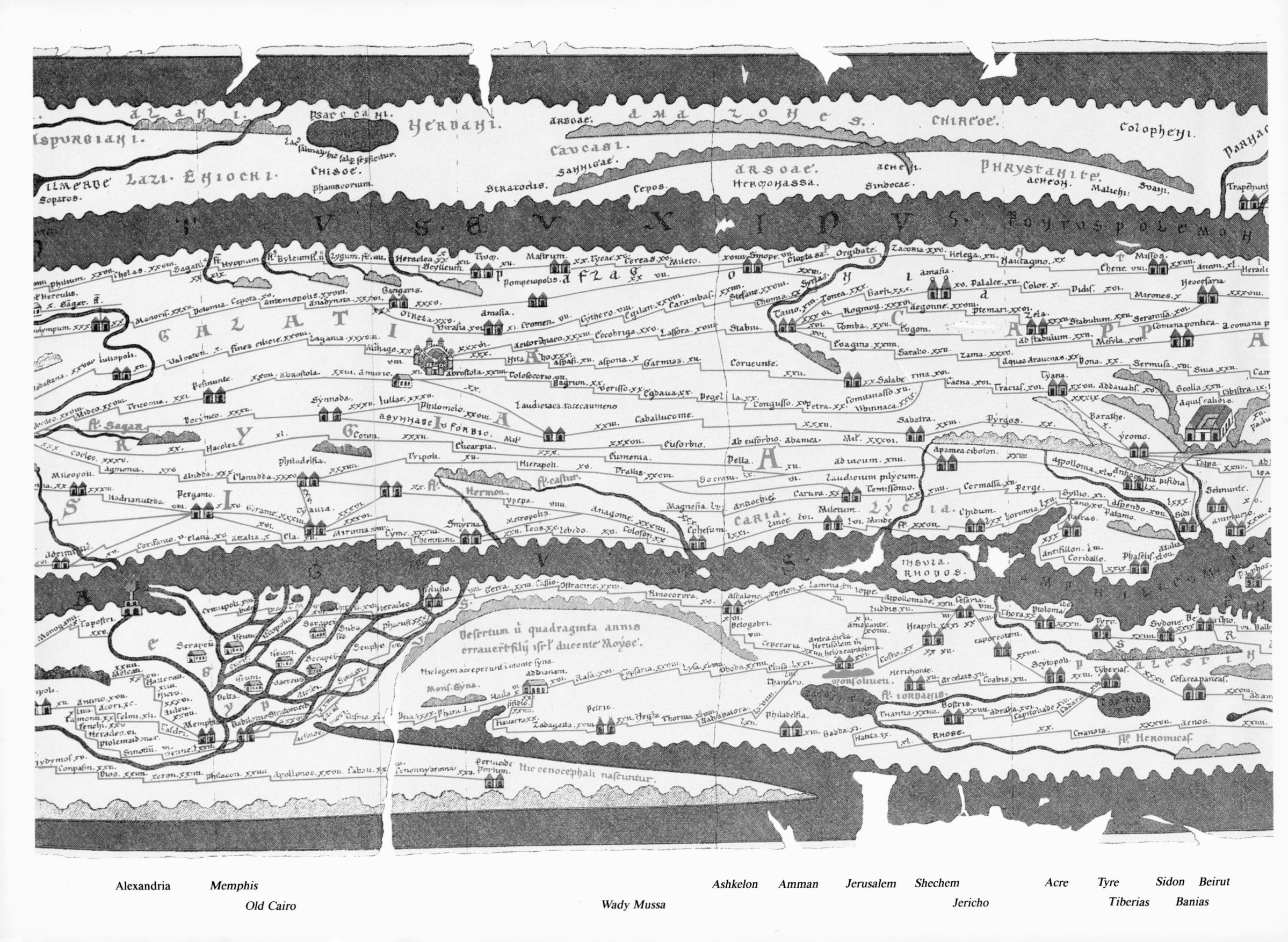

Alexandria   Memphis   Ashkelon Amman Jerusalem Shechem   Acre Tyre Sidon Beirut

Old Cairo   *Wady Mussa*   *Jericho*   *Tiberias* *Banias*

Relief showing Roman legionaries.

Ancient Roman road,
located off present Beit Horon road (east of Kfar Ruth junction).

The Peutinger Map

This map – a road map of the Roman Empire – takes its name from the German map collector Conrad Peutinger (1465-1547). Peutinger received this map, a manuscript of the twelfth or thirteenth century, from Conrad Celtes, and copied only two sections of it. The copy shown here is based on the 1653 edition by Jan Janson.

It is estimated that this map was copied from an ancient map apparently drawn around 365 C.E. It describes the roads of the Roman Empire from Gaul in the west to India in the east. The map takes the form of a long, narrow parchment scroll (approximately 33 x 682 cm.), divided into twelve sections. Section one, the extreme west, was lost. The Land of Israel appears in section eleven. There, as in the rest of the map, important settlements are noted, with distances between them marked in Roman miles.

Jerusalem is depicted by two buildings and the Mount of Olives. Above it appears the inscription: "Formerly called Jerusalem (and today) Aelia Capitolina". One of the roads leaving Jerusalem crosses the Negev Desert and ends at Elat on the shores of the Red Sea. Among other sites mentioned on the map are the Jordan River, Tiberias, The Dead Sea, Jaffa, Ptolemaida ('Akko), Azoton (Ashdod) and Ascalon (Ashqelon).

In an attempt to accommodate the entire Empire in a narrow scroll, the cartographer had to make the map narrow. To do so he reduced the areas of the sea to narrow strips. As a result, many lines running north-south are sketched in the map from right to left. The proper dimensions for east-west are largely maintained. The Peutinger Map probably served travellers to the Land of Israel, including pilgrims.

The following story is told about the Roman road from Jerusalem to Elat: During the War of Independence in 1948 the Israeli High Command had a secret plan to conquer the Negev and Elat. This plan was called "Operation Fact". Yigael Yadin, the chief of operations and an archaeologist by profession, knew of the Roman road leading from Jerusalem to Elat – shown in the Peutinger Map – parts of which had been preserved under the desert sand.

The armoured column sent to conquer Elat followed this route and reached the shores of the Red Sea. In doing so, they caught the enemy by surprise, for the Jordanians did not believe that the Israeli army would succeed in crossing the desert in the absence of a partly paved road.

LANDMARKS OF THE ERA

IMP·TITI IVDAICVS TRIVMPHVS

·MENSA AVREA CVM·CYATHIS LIBAMINVM ET·TVBIS HYMNODIARVM·CANDELABRVM EX AVRO FACTVM·EQVES PHALERIS ORNATVS HABET CINGVLVM IN PECTO

RE CVM CLAVICVLIS AVREIS·Silius Ital. Phaleris hic pectore fulget·QVIRITES ALBA VESTE INDVTI LAVRV CORONATI LAVRV MANV FERENTES CVRRV PRAECEDVT Praecedentia longi Agminis officia

Peter Sanct. Bartol. delin-et sculp·   In Arcu Titi

Prisoners from Judea carrying the vessels of the Temple, in Titus' triumphal march.
Copper engraving, eighteenth century.

vic:oziam non bumane virtutis sed diuine gratie fateretur. In ea vastatione fuit ea bominū strages ea fa-
mes miseroz funesta necessitas: Que si ex ordine noscere cupis Josephum lege. non audita sed visa et cōm-
munia sibi cū ceteris referente. Uenies deuicz Tit⁹ romā cū patre suo Uespasiano triumphū celeberrimuz
egit. Simone qui vrbis excidij causa fuit in trūpbo pductū postea laqueo p totā ciuitate traxerunt multis
confossiuz vulnerib⁹ interfecerūt. Uespasian⁹ templū pacis edificauit vbi iudeoz preciosioza instrumēta vi
delicet tabulas legis penetraliū vela. z alia multa reposuit. Ea aūt vrbs vsqz ad adriani principis tpa la-
tronū sicarioruqz facta est receptaculū. Et p quiquagita annos: deinde ciuitatis māsere reliquie. Quā postea Adrianus impatoz menib⁹ z edificijs instaurās de suo noie belyam appellauit: et diu⁹ Hieronim⁹ ad

QUinta seculi etas Hic incipit et oztum habuit a captiuitate iudeozum in Babiloniam duratqz vicz
ad christi iesu domini nostri natiuitatem per annos. 590. quis in hac supputatione aliqui aliter
sentiant. Unde qui recte captiuitatis annos numerare voluerint ab vndecimo Sedechie regni anno vt Eusebius ponit. tunc septuaginta captiuitatis annos in secūdū Barij annuz terminabunt. Joseph⁹
et diuus Hieronimus a. ij. Josie regis vsqz ad tercium Cyri regis annus. Nonnulli ab vltimo regis Joa-
chim anno computant vsqz ad vltimum Cyri annum. At sane sentiendo septuaginta illi anni qui in tercio
vel vltimo Cyri anno terminantur. propzie captiuitatis iudaice anni dicuntur. Illi vero qui in scdo Barij
terminantur propzie complete transmigratiōis sunt. Et hec principalioz et precipua sacre scripture era ba

The destruction of Jerusalem.
From the book by H. Schedel, 1492.

43

c. 600

COLOURED STONES

Section of floor mosaic
from a synagogue in Bet Guvrin, fifth century.

45

Arculf

Church of the Holy Sepulchre.
From the Book of Bernhardt
von Breydenbach, 1486.

Arculf, (or Arculfus) was a French bishop in the seventh century C.E. who travelled to the Holy Land and toured it for about nine months.

Opinions vary regarding the date of his visit there. Presumably it took place sometime between the years 670 and the end of 697. In those days the land was ruled by the Caliphs of the Umayyad dynasty.

On concluding his tour of the Holy Land, Arculf planned to return home. However his ship was swept ashore on the isle of Iona in Scotland. There he recounted the tales of his travels to the abbot of the local monastery, who duly recorded them in an essay titled "De Locis Sanctis" ("Of the Holy Places").

In this essay Arculf describes the several months he spent in Jerusalem, adding detailed descriptions of the Christian holy sites.

He also visited Nazareth, Capernaum, Mt. Tabor and Bethlehem, describing the graves of the patriarchs in Hebron, and the grave of Adam "on which rests a dark-hued stone...". The chapter on his journey to Jericho includes a fascinating description on how salt is derived from the Dead Sea. Arculf is thought to have been the first Christian traveller who toured the Near East following the Moslem occupation, and for many generations his descriptions constituted an important source of information on the holy sites for Christian pilgrims.

"...Arculf, the holy bishop, a native of Gaul, after visiting many remote countries, resided nine months at Jerusalem, and made daily visits to the surrounding districts. He counted in the circuit of the walls of the holy city eighty-four towers and six gates..."

(His personal description of his travels was recorded by Adamnan,
Abbot of the monastery at Iona, in his book
"The Travels of Bishop Arculf in the Holy Land." c. 700 C.E.)

HIERVSALEM

Jerusalem, part of mosaic
in the church of San Vitale of Ravenna, 540.

On the spot where the Temple once stood, near the eastern wall, the Saracens have now erected a square house of prayer, in a rough manner, by raising beams and planks upon some remains of old ruins; this is their place of worship, and it is said that it will hold about three thousand men.

Between these two churches is the place where Abraham raised the altar for the sacrifice of his son Isaac, where there is now a small wooden table on which the alms for the poor are offered.

...On the highest point of Mount Olivet, where our Lord ascended into heaven, is a large round church, having around it three vaulted porticoes. In the western part of the same church are eight windows; and eight lamps, hanging by cords opposite them, cast their light through the glass as far as Jerusalem; which light, Arculf said, strikes the hearts of the beholders with a mixture of joy and divine fear. Every year, on the day of the Ascension, when mass is ended, a strong blast of wind comes down, and casts to the ground all who are in the church. All that night, lanterns are kept burning there, so that the mountain appears not only lighted up, but actually on fire, and all that side of the city is illuminated by it.

...There is a highway, according to Arculf, leading southward from Jerusalem to Hebron, to the east of which Bethlehem is situated, six miles from Jerusalem. At the extremity of this road, on the west side, is the tomb of Rachel, crudely built of stones, without any ornament, presenting externally the form of a pyramid. Her name, placed there by her husband Jacob is still shown upon it. Hebron, which is also called Mamre, has no walls, and exhibits only the ruins of the ancient city; but there are some ill-built villages and hamlets scattered over the plain, and inhabited by a multitude of people. To the east is a double cave, looking toward Mamre, where are the tombs of the four patriarchs, Abram, Isaac, Jacob, and Adam the first man. Contrary to the usual custom, they are placed with the feet to the south, and the head to the north; and they are inclosed by a square low wall. Each of the tombs is covered with a single stone, worked somewhat in form of a church, and of a light colour for those of three patriarchs, which are together. Arculf also saw poorer and smaller monuments of the three women, Sarah, Rebecca, and Leah, who were here buried in the earth.

...In another excursion, Arculf proceeded to Jericho, where although the city had been three times built, and as many times utterly destroyed, yet the walls of the house of Rahab still stand, although without a roof. A large church stands on the site of Galgalis, where the children of Israel first encamped after passing the Jordan. It is five miles from Jericho. Within the church are the twelve stones which Joshua ordered to be taken out of the Jordan; six on the south side of the church floor, and six on the north. They are so heavy, that two strong men, at the present day, could hardly lift one of them"...

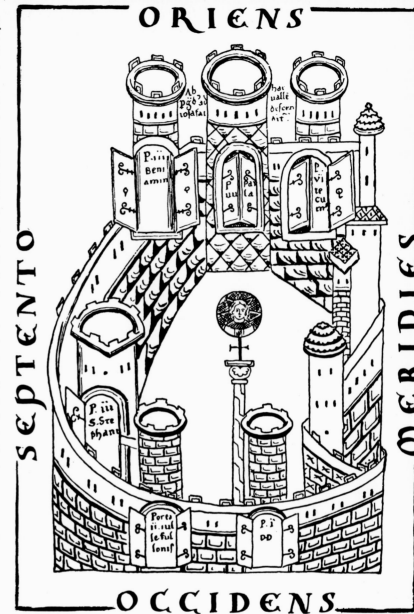

Map of Jerusalem.
From the travel book of Arculf, c.700.

Arculf

(From "Travels of Bishop Arculf in the Holy Land", c. 700 C.E.)

47

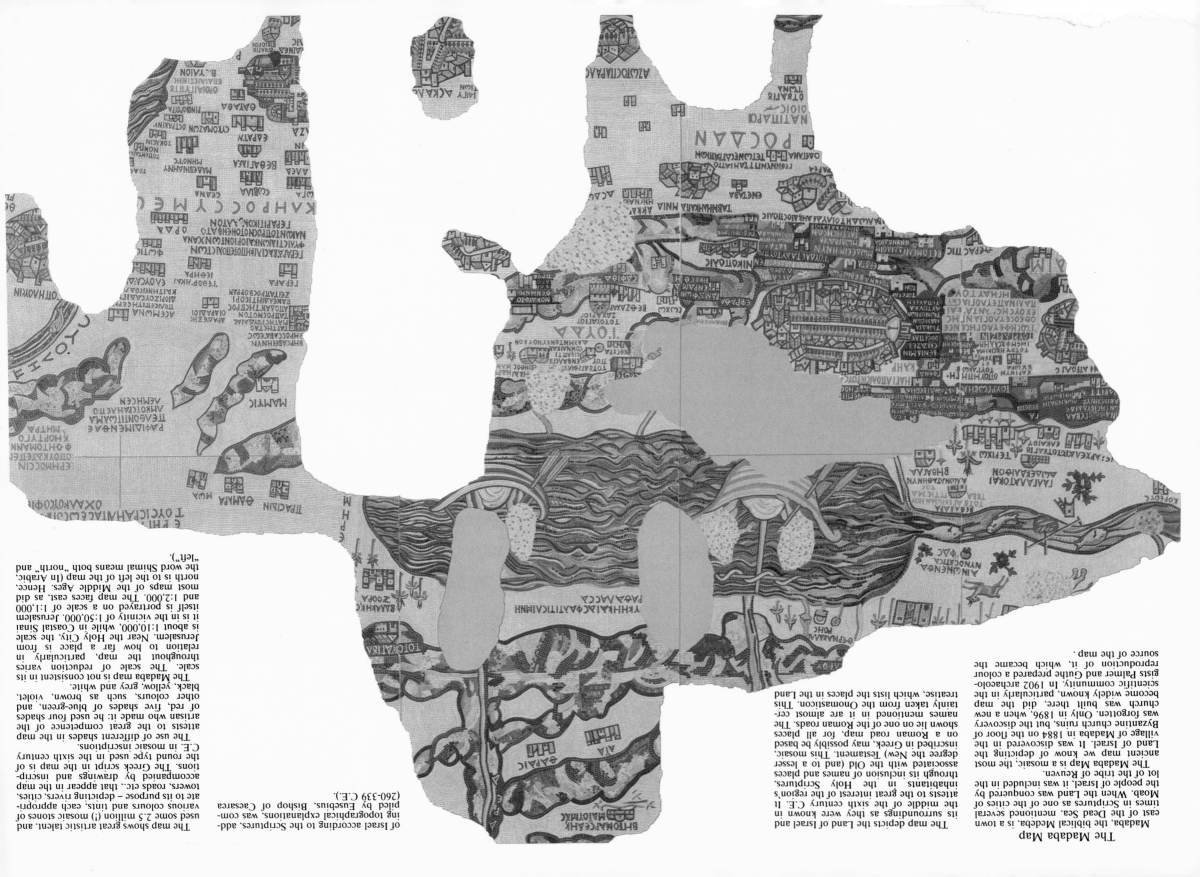

The Madaba Map

Madaba, the biblical Medeba, is a town east of the Dead Sea, mentioned several times in Scriptures as they were known in its surroundings. Moab. When the Land was conquered by the people of Israel, it was included in the lot of the tribe of Reuven.

The Madaba Map is a mosaic, the most ancient map we know of depicting the Land of Israel. It was discovered in the Byzantine church ruins, but the discovery was forgotten. Only in 1896, when a new church was built there, did the map become widely known, particularly in the scientific community. In 1902 archaeologists Palmer and Guthe prepared a colour reproduction of it, which became the source of the map.

The map depicts the Land of Israel and its surroundings as they were known in the middle of the sixth century C.E. It attests to the great interest of the region's inhabitants in the Holy Scriptures, through its inclusion of names and places associated with the Old (and to a lesser degree the New) Testament. This mosaic, inscribed in Greek, may possibly be based on a Roman road map, for all places shown lie on one of the Roman roads. The names mentioned in it are almost certainly taken from the Onomasticon. This treatise, which lists the places in the Land of Israel according to the Scriptures, adding topographical explanations, was compiled by Eusebius, Bishop of Caesarea (260-339 C.E.).

The map shows great artistic talent, and used some 2.5 million (!) mosaic stones of various colours and tints, each appropriate to its purpose – depicting rivers, cities, towers, roads etc. that appear in the map accompanied by drawings and inscriptions. The Greek script in the map is of the round type used in the sixth century C.E. in mosaic inscriptions.

The use of different shades in the map attests to the great competence of the artisan who made it: he used four shades of red, five shades of blue-green, and other colours, such as brown, violet, black, yellow, grey and white.

The Madaba map is not consistent in its scale. The scale of reduction varies throughout the map, particularly in relation to how far a place is from Jerusalem. Near the Holy City, the scale is about 1:10,000, while in Coastal Sinai it is in the vicinity of 1:50,000. Jerusalem itself is portrayed on a scale of 1:1,000 and 1:2,000. The map faces east, as did most maps of the Middle Ages. Hence, north is to the left of the map (In Arabic, the word Shimal means both "north" and "left").

Jerusalem

Jericho

Bethlehem

Depiction of Jerusalem in the Madaba Map

Jerusalem is portrayed in the centre of the map. It appears as it was in the sixth century C.E., and is shown in oval form, in west-to-east bird's-eye view. The map bears many details of Jerusalem, chiefly involving its walls, gates, public buildings and churches. To the present day, at least forty-eight structures have been identified.

The city's central thoroughfare passes in a straight line from left to right, i.e. from north to south. This is the Cardo, (Latin for "axis"). This street is open at its right end. At the northern (left) edge of the city, Damascus Gate can be seen and next to it is depicted the pillar which marked the starting point for measuring distances in the Land of Israel during the Byzantine period (the Arabic name, Bab el-'Ammud, "Gate of the Pillar", alludes to this.) In the centre, west of the Cardo, the Church of the Holy Sepulchre can be seen. The structure at the southern-right end is the "New Church" (Nea).

Jericho

Jericho is one of the most ancient cities in the world. It is particularly known for its mighty walls, which, according to the Scriptures, fell at the sound of the ram's horn during the conquest by Joshua. The importance of Jericho stems from its strategic location on a route leading from the eastern side of the Jordan to the Land of Israel and its coastal cities.

Jericho was an impressive city. The palaces of wealthy Jerusalemites crowned it during most of the periods in which it was inhabited. Its near surroundings were fertile, and its agriculture was well tended thanks to numerous springs. Date palms heavy with fruit encompass Jericho on all sides. This is why Jericho is also known as "The City of Dates".

Bethlehem

As the story goes, the source of Bethlehem's name is the bread, (lehem in Hebrew), baked by its inhabitants. This story seems to be associated with the Scriptural tale of Ruth the Moabite, who gathered sheaves in the field of Boaz.

Bethlehem is further mentioned in the tales of the Patriarchs. Rachel, the wife of Jacob, died and was buried "on the way to Efrat, at Bethlehem" (Genesis 35:19). Tradition holds that the Messiah is destined to rise up for the Jewish people out of the seed of King David, and David, a fifth generation descendant of Boaz and Ruth, was born there as well.

As the New Testament relates, the Christian Messiah Jesus, the son of Mary, was also born in Bethlehem. The church father Hieronymus, who translated the Bible into Latin (the "Vulgate" translation), lived in Bethlehem at the end of the fourth century C.E. In the Madaba map Bethlehem is marked to the right, i.e. to the south of Jerusalem, in red letters, as befits an important and famous city. In Bethlehem we can see two towers and a large structure with a red dome. This is the Church of the Nativity, first built in the Byzantine period.

LANDMARKS OF THE ERA

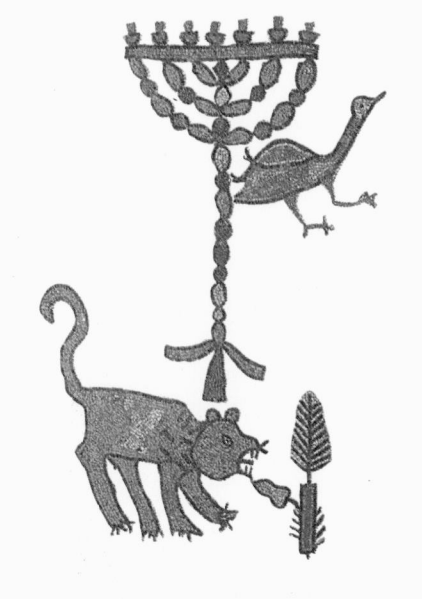

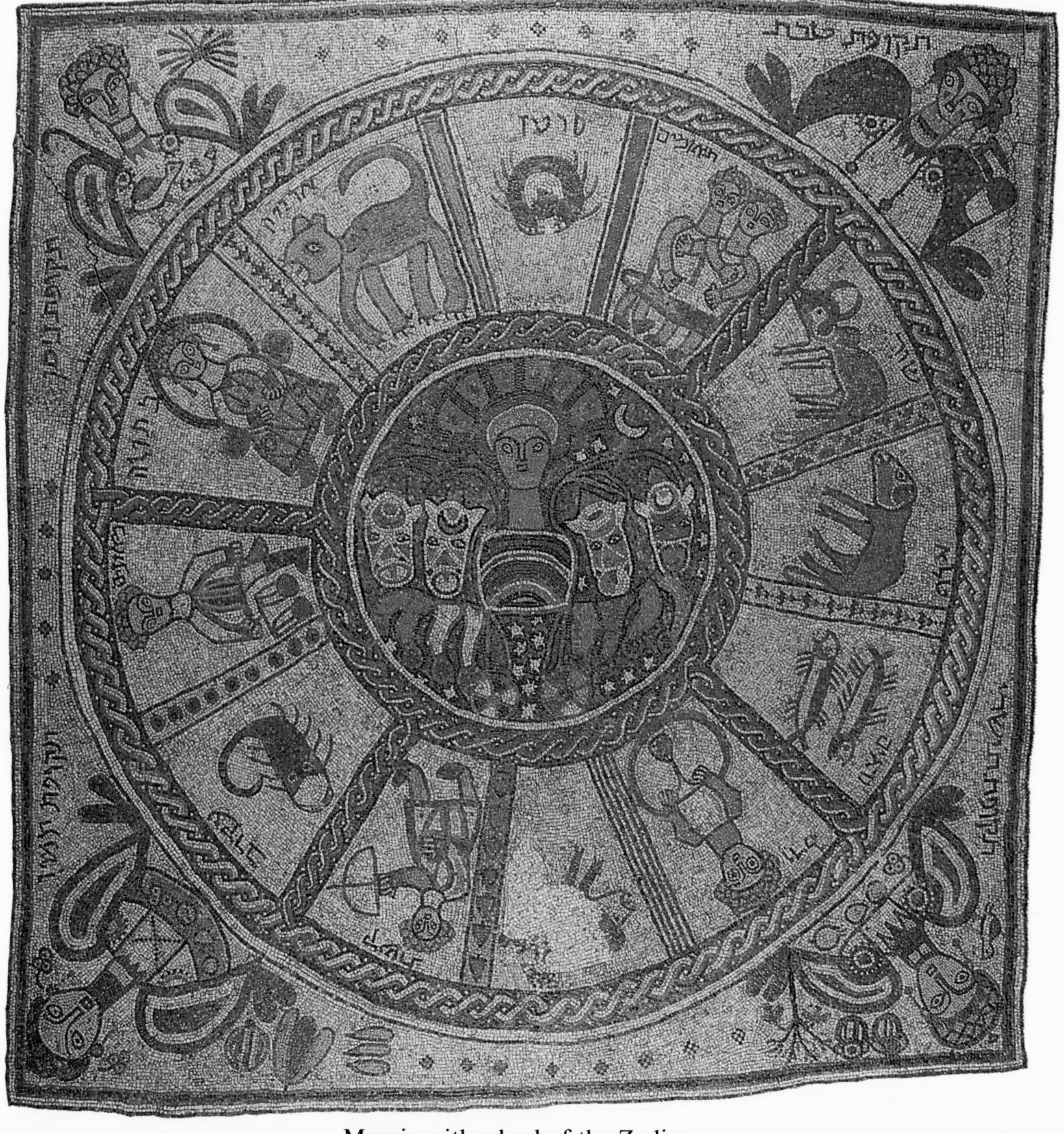

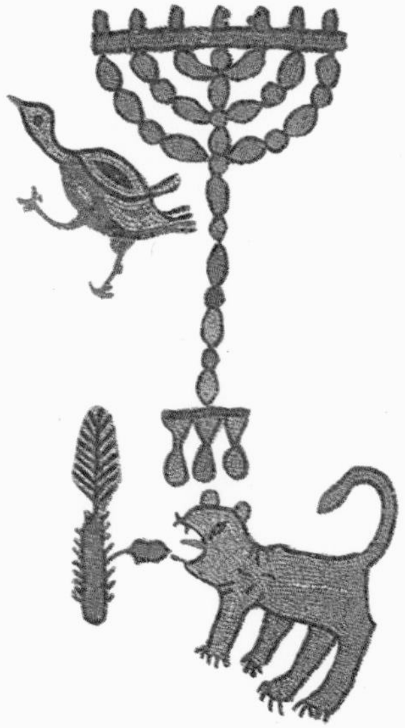

Mosaic with wheel of the Zodiac.
In the centre – Helios, the God of sun.
Floor of Beit Alfa synagogue, sixth century.

Mosaic of animals, lioness.
Church near Kissufim, sixth century.

Mosaic of panther hunt.
Church near Kissufim, sixth century.

Mosaic of birds, centaur and flowers.
Floor of Roman villa in Nablus, third century.

Mosaic panel with medallion of human head
Floor of Roman villa in Nablus, third century.

1099-1250

WARRIORS OF FAITH

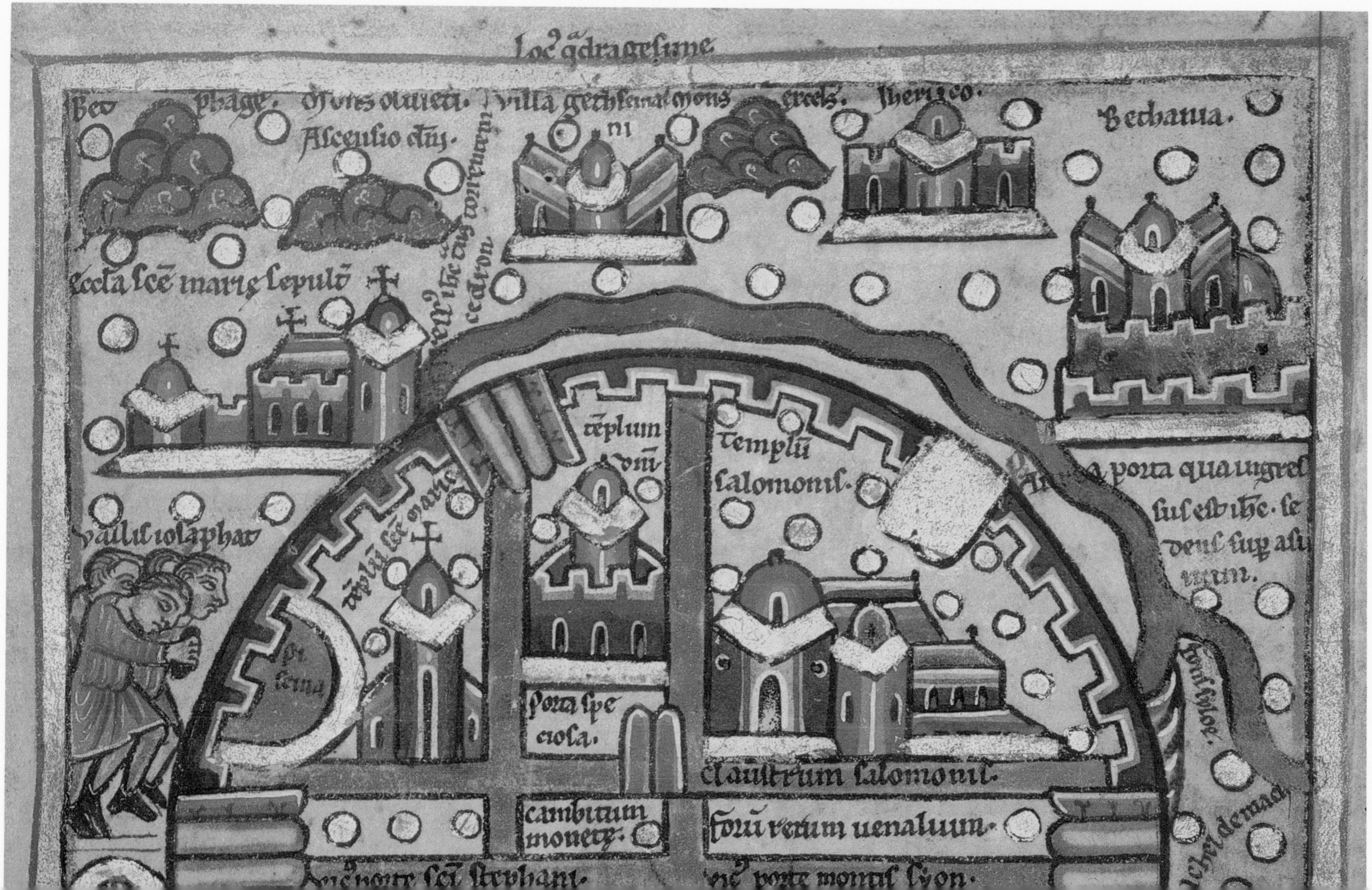

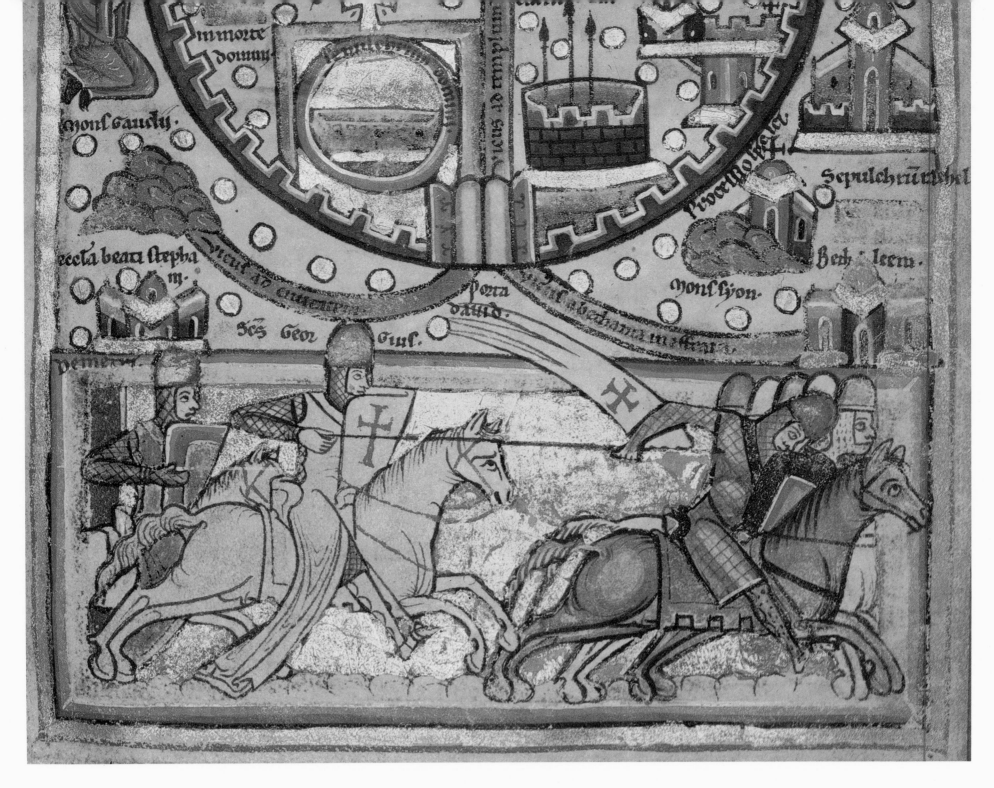

Jerusalem
from a Crusader's manuscript, c. 1170.

53

Rabbi Benjamin of Tudela

מסעות של רבי בנימן זל

Title-page
of Rabbi Benjamin of Tudela's treatise,
printed in Ferrara, Italy, 1556.

Rabbi Benjamin, who lived in the 12th century, was one of the most important Jewish pilgrims of the Middle Ages. He was born in Tudela, in the Navarra region of Spain, and set out on his travels in 1165. He passed through southern France, Italy and Greece. He sailed from Constantinople to Antioch, and from there reached the Holy Land via Syria in 1170. Benjamin of Tudela traveled across the land from Acre to Jerusalem, from there up to the Jordan Valley and north, and then via Safed, back into Syria. In those days all the coastal towns of the Holy Land were ruled by the Crusaders. In 1187 Saladin defeated the Crusaders and merged the Holy Land, Syria and Egypt, bringing them all under Moslem rule.

Jewish settlement in the Holy Land was sparse in those days, numbering only some 2000 families, living mainly in the towns, among them some 1000 Samarian families living in the vicinity of Nablus. His book provides geographical descriptions of the places visited by Rabbi Benjamin and reviews the way of life of the Jewish communities in the various countries through which he had travelled. The book serves as an important source of information on the Mediterranean countries in the Middle Ages and on the condition of dispersed Jewry in those times, as well as on the history of the Holy Land during the Crusades.

"...This book contains the reports of Rabbi Benjamin, the son of Jonah of blessed memory, of Tudela, in the kingdom of Navarra. This man travelled through many and distant countries, as related in the following account, and took down in writing in each place what he saw or what was told him by men of integrity, whose names were known in Spain... Rabbi Benjamin was a man of wisdom and understanding, and of much information; and after strict inquiry his words were found to be true and correct, for he was a true man..."

(Words of the copyist.
Preface to "The Travels of Rabbi Benjamin of Tudela in the Land of Israel", c. 1170.)

Absalom's Pillar.
Lithography by David Roberts, 1839.

"From thence it is three parasangs to Jerusalem, a small city strongly fortified with three walls. It contains a numerous population, composed of Jacobites, Armenians, Greeks, Georgians, Franks, and indeed of people of all tongues. The dyeing-house is rented by the year, and exclusive privilege of dyeing is purchased from the king by the Jews of Jerusalem, two hundred of whom dwell in one corner of the city, under the tower of David. About ten yards of the base of this building are very ancient, having been constructed by our ancestors; the remaining part was added by the Mohammedans. The city contains no building stronger than the tower of David. There are at Jerusalem two hospices, which support four hundred knights, and afford shelter to the sick; these are provided with every thing they may want, both during life and in death; the second is called the hospital of Solomon, being the palace originally built by king Solomon. This hospice also harbours and furnishes four hundred knights, who are ever ready to wage war, over and above those knights who arrive from the country of the Franks and other parts of Christendom. These generally have taken a vow upon themselves to stay a year or two, and they remain until the period of their vow is expired. The large place of worship, called Sepulchre, and containing the sepulchre of that man, is visited by all pilgrims.

Jerusalem has four gates, called the gates of Abraham, David, Sion, and Jehoshaphat. The latter stands opposite the place of the holy Temple, which is occupied at present by a building called Templum Domini. Omar ben al-Khatab erected a large handsome cupola over it, and nobody is allowed to introduce any image or painting into this place, it being set aside for prayers only. In front of it you see the Western Wall, one of the walls which formed the Holy of Holies of the ancient temple; it is called the Gate of Mercy, and all Jews resort thither to say their prayers near the wall of the courtyard. At Jerusalem you also see the stables erected by Solomon, which formed part of his house. Immense stones have been employed in this fabric, the like of which are nowhere else to be met with. You further see to this day vestiges of the canal near which the sacrifices were slaughtered in ancient times; and all Jews inscribe their name upon an adjacent wall. If you leave the city by the gate of Jehoshaphat, you may see the pillar erected on Absalom's place, and the sepulchre of King Uzziah, and the great spring of Shiloah, which runs into the brook Kidron. Over this spring is a large building erected in the times of our forefathers. Very little water is found at Jerusalem; the inhabitants generally drink rain water, which they collect in their houses."

Jerusalem.
Detail from a map by Rabbi S. Pinie.

Benjamin of Tudela

(From "Travels of Rabbi Benjamin of Tudela in the Land of Israel", c. 1170.)

The Psalter Map

The Map

The map was attached to a thirteenth century manuscript of the Book of Psalms, hence its name, "The Psalter Map".

This is a circular world map with an O-T (Orbis Terrarum) layout, such as characterized mediaeval maps. In it, the world is divided into three parts, each containing one of the three then-known continents: Europe, Asia and Africa. At the centre of the world is the Land of Israel, and at its hub, Jerusalem. This concept stems from the Christian outlook of the map makers, who usually emphasized two important sites – Jerusalem and the Garden of Eden.

In the O-T maps, oriented to the east, the Garden of Eden, described in Genesis as lying to the east, if shown, appears at the top of the map. The Mediterranean Sea comprises the vertical line of the letter T. The Red Sea or the river Nile divides between Africa and Asia (and the Land of Israel in particular). The rest of the seas and their islands appear in the surrounding portion of the map.

The Garden of Eden

Near the top of the map, i.e. in the east, there is a picture of the Garden of Eden, with typical drawings of Adam and Eve, and the Tree of Knowledge between them. Out of Eden flow the four Scriptural rivers, Pishon, Gihon, Tigris and Euphrates, as well as the River Ganges.

Africa

The African continent was little known in this period. Hence, its description was based on oral testimony, and on the reports of Roman and Greek scribes who allowed their imagination full reign when describing it.

For example, Solinus Gaius Julius, a Roman scribe of the third century C.E., wrote a book which was later adapted into a collection entitled "Polyhistor". It contained a historical, religious, and social description of the ancient world. In this work he described the inhabitants of continental Africa as mythical beings with two heads, women with beards, men with four eyes or one foot.

These fanciful descriptions were copied, and were made even more colourful in the course of time. Every artist added something of his own. We also find these drawings in the southern (right) part of the "Psalter Map", where Africa is shown.

Frederick II
"King of Jerusalem and Sicily"

Crusader king in Jerusalem. From a fourteenth century French manuscript.

Frederick II of the House of Hohenstaufen (1194-1250), Emperor of the Holy Roman Empire, King of Sicily and Jerusalem, led the fifth Crusade to the Holy Land, landing on the shores of Acre on 7th September,1228. Following a treaty signed by him and the Turkish Sultan in February 1229, he obtained the peaceful cession of Jerusalem, Bethlehem, Nazareth and its environs to the Christians.

He was crowned King of Jerusalem in the Holy Sepulchre on March 18, 1229.
Frederick II was an educated man, fluent in six languages. His court in Palermo, Sicily was an enlightened and vibrant cultural centre. Aided by Christian, Moslem and Jewish scholars of his court, Frederick II founded the first University in Naples in 1224.

"...The baronies and their dependencies were obliged to furnish two thousand horse; and the cities of Jerusalem, Acre and Naplusia, six hundred and sixty-six horse, and one hundred and thirteen foot; The Towns of Ascalon, Tyre, Caesarea and Tiberias, a thousand foot...".

(From an account of "The Kingdom of Jerusalem" by Abbe A. Guenée, 1780.)

Departure of Godfrey, King of France by ship on the first Crusade.
From a fourteenth century French manuscript.

The Ebstorf Map

Further to his other titles, Frederick II of the House of Hohenstaufen was also known as King of Sicily and Jerusalem. He was eager to recapture the Kingdom of Jerusalem from the Moslem infidels as early as 1220, and to this end he tried to persuade other European rulers to join him in a new Crusade to free the Holy Land. However, Frederick II's voyage was postponed following a clash between him and Pope Honorius III.

Eventually, in 1225 Frederick II, in an attempt to conciliate the Pope, pledged to "maintain one thousand knights in the Holy Land for two years, to place one hundred merchant vessels and fifty ships at the disposal of the Crusaders, and to assist two thousand additional Crusaders to reach the Holy Land".

Nevertheless it was not until 1227 that knights and equipment from other European countries joined Frederick II. Once again his voyage had to be postponed owing to the Emperor's ill-health and to the plague that had meanwhile beset his army.

The Crusade began on June 28, 1228 when a fleet of forty vessels, led by the King, left Brindisi, Italy for the Holy Land.

The Ebstorf World Map

The Ebstorf World Map was discovered in 1830 in a Benedictine monastery in the town of Ebstorf, south of Hamburg. It was apparently drawn by an English monk, Gervasius of Tilbury, and appended to the treatise "Solacium Imperatoris", which was later to be called "Olia Imperalia".

This treatise reviewed world history and the lives of the great men. It was written and designed in Sicily in the thirteenth century, at the court of the German King Frederick II of the House of Hohenstaufen, and it was he who ordered the making of the map.

The size of the original map, drawn on parchment, is 3.58 x 3.56 m. As in other maps bearing the O-T structure (Orbis Terrarum – "sphere of the earth"), the O describing the circumference of the map represents the oceans, while the T divides between the three then-known continents. In the upper part is Asia. Europe is shown to the left and Africa to the right. In the center of many O-T type maps are found the Holy Land and Jerusalem.

In the Ebstorf Map Jesus is depicted as creating or embracing the world. In Asia we find the Garden of Eden, containing Adam, Eve and the serpent.

To the right, in the Middle-East, depicted in the central portion of the map, we find the empires of the ancient world, Assyria and Babylon, as well as the Land of Israel. The latter is shown in relative detail: Galilee, Samaria, the Sea of Genesareth (Kinneret) and its fish, the Jordan river, and many cities mentioned in the Bible. Egypt is found to the right, i.e. south, of the Land of Israel.

In the African continent, on the right side of the map, we find pictorial representations of the various peoples that live there, as well as of its animals and birds, most of them imaginary. In Europe, at the bottom left part of the map, are described the great kingdoms of that period: England, France (Francia), Germany (Teutonia), Scotland (Scotia), and others. Included are drawings of important cities, rivers, and even of large castles.

Capture of Jerusalem by the Crusaders in 1099.
From a fourteenth century French manuscript.

Frederick II

Monialium Ebstorfensium Mappamundi

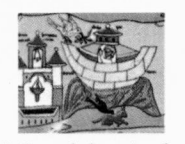

Noah's Ark

Noah built his ark when commanded by the Lord to save himself and his family as well as one male and one female of each species of beast in Creation, from a flood which the Lord would bring down upon the earth.

The ark is shown on the mountains of Ararat, where it came to rest when the flood waters had subsided. Also shown is Noah sending forth a dove "to see if the waters were abated from off the face of the ground".

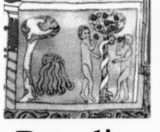

Paradise

Home of Adam, the first man, paradise is portrayed in detail in maps of the world drawn in the 13th - 15th centuries. Most of these contain a description of Adam and Eve by the tree of knowledge, with temptation in form of the serpent and apple, as well as the four rivers running through paradise - the Gihon, Pishon, Tigris and Euphrates.

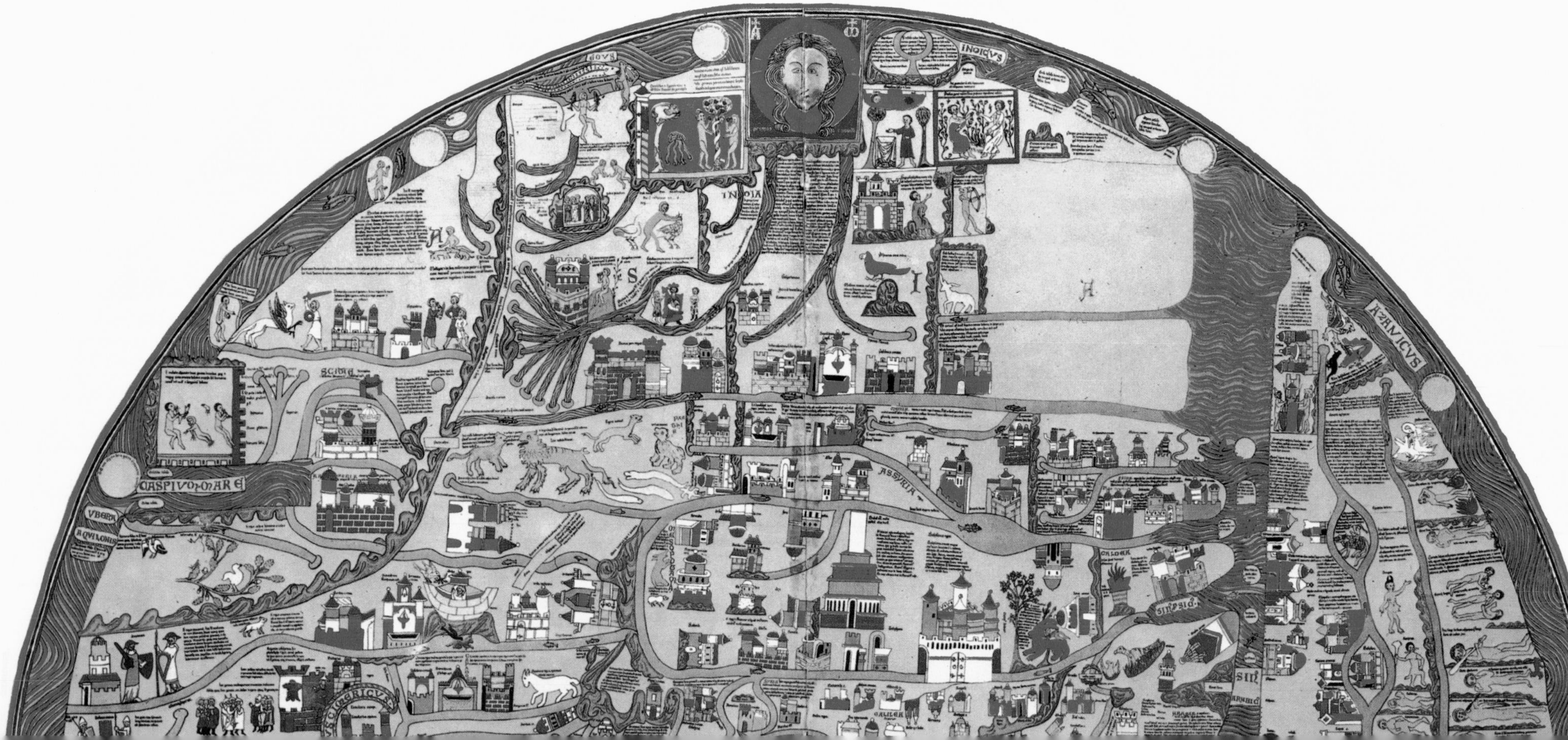

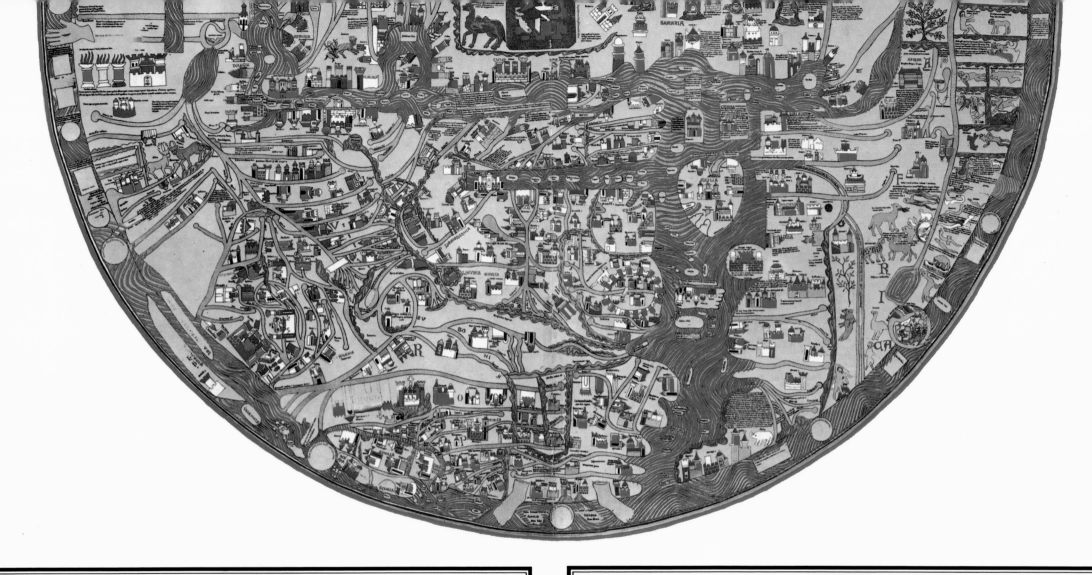

Venice

Principal port on the Adriatic coast. Between the 11th and 15th centuries Venice was an important point of departure for crusaders embarking for the Holy Land, as well as a focal mercantile and trading centre with other Mediterranean countries.

The Venetians obtained the right to berth their vessels and build naval bases in various port towns in the Holy Land and to the north - Acre, Tyre and Sidon.

Here Venice is shown surrounded by walled fortifications and bisected by the Grand Canal. Also shown is the emblem of the city, the lion of San Marco, Venice's patron saint (St. Mark).

Sicily

The largest island in the Mediterranean is depicted here in form of a heart, in appreciation of Emperor Frederick II of Hohenstaufen, King of Sicily. Sicily was an important cultural centre from the 12th to the 15th century. Its inhabitants consisted of Moslem, Greeks, Italians and Jews. Their different cultures all flourished and prospered in the court of the enlightened Frederick II, patron of the arts and sciences. Numerous treatises were written during this period on biology, philosophy and poetry, and translations of important ancient cultural works were published.

It should be noted that Sicily's Jewish population enjoyed full civic rights and privileges. As subjects of Frederick II the Jews were protected from persecution and oppression.

61

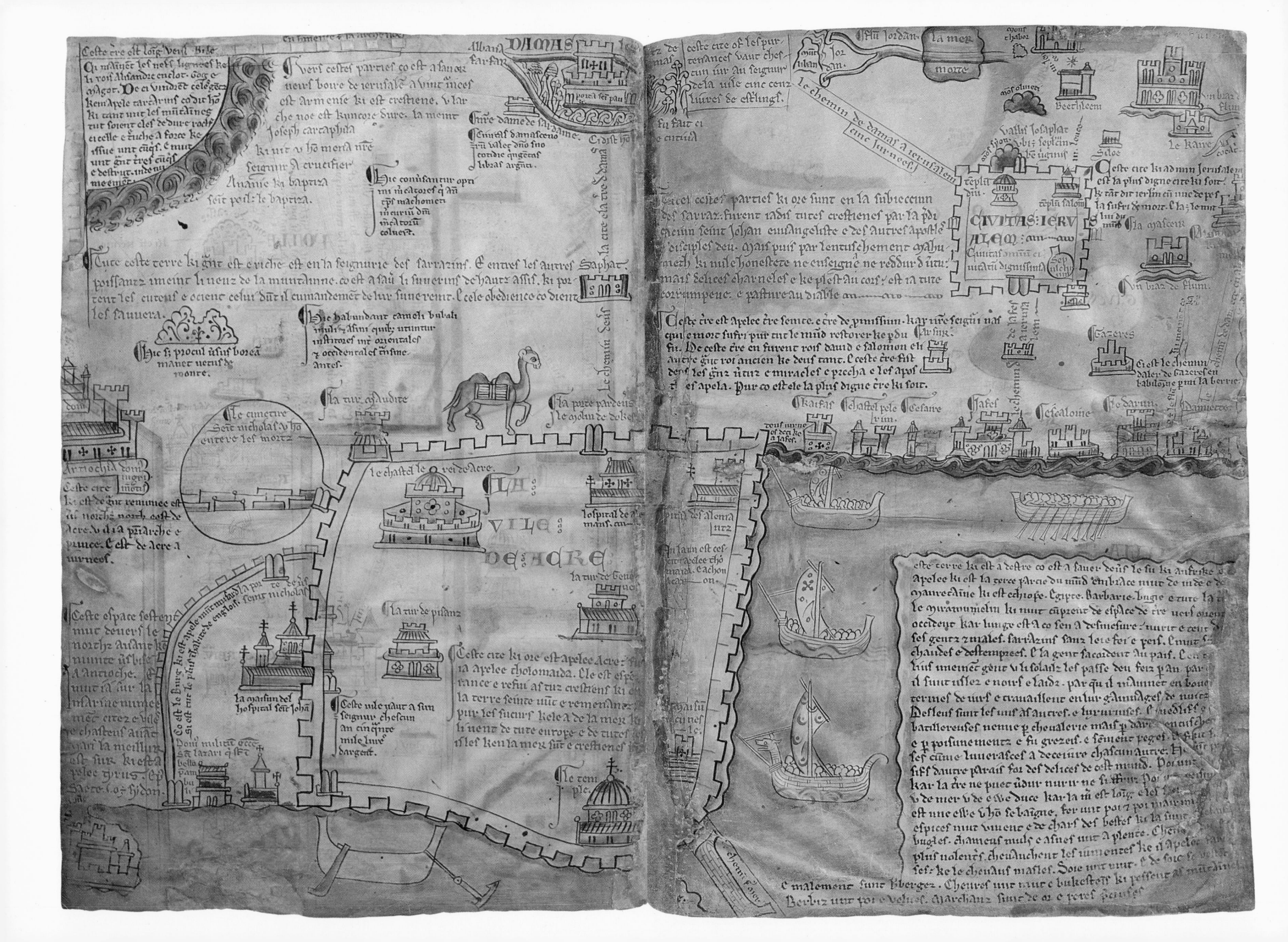

Jerusalem is depicted in the upper part of the right page, inside a square wall with the inscription:"Civitas Hiervsalem". Conspicuous are the Church of the Holy Sepulchre, the Temple of Solomon (Templu Salom), and in the east – the "Valley of Jehoshafat".
Jaffa gate is seen in the west with the road leading from Jerusalem to Jaffa . In the north-east; a mention of the road leading from Jerusalem to Damascus.

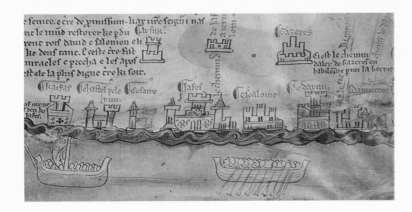

The coastal cities of the Holy Land; Haifa, Atlit, Caesarea, Jaffa and Askalon are mentioned in great detail. Various types of vessels are shown in the Sea.

Map of Matthew Paris
The Crusader Kingdom of Jerusalem.

The Crusaders' rule over the Holy Land lasted less than 200 years, from the day in July 1099 when Jerusalem was captured by the religion-motivated warriors who had come from Europe. In addition to numerous city maps, especially of Jerusalem and Akko (Acre), we also find maps of the entire country, and even a map of the route from Europe to the Holy Land for the benefit of pilgrims. One of the most versatile documented artists of the period was Matthew Paris, a monk of St. Albans near London, who was a chronicler both in words and illustrations. Paris' "Chronica maiora" was accompanied by several maps. One of these, drawn around the year 1250, is reproduced here. It depicts Palestine, the Latin Kingdom of Jerusalem in its later stages which already give evidence of the decay which led to its demise. Thus Jerusalem, drawn as a square of walls, occupies only 1/13th the area of Acre, which supplanted the Holy City as capital after the latter was retaken by the Moslems.

The ratio of these areas undoubtedly reflects the transfer of the administrative, military and political center of gravity to Acre. Paris apparently never visited the country, and his maps as well as his verbal descriptions were based on information received from travellers. This accounts for the sharply angled coastline with its exaggerated representation of the Bay of Acre (today's Haifa Bay), in which both Christian and Moslem ships are shown – sailing vessels as well as oar-propelled ships. The twin-humped camel shown near the Acre city wall is not found in this region, and must have been transplanted there from inner Asia. Within the city confines many of the public institutions are drawn and named.

Maimonides
(Rabbi Moses ben Maimon)

Rabbi Moshe Ben Maimon (Maimonides), known by his initials as the Rambam (1135-1204) was a highly gifted and versatile personage – one of the great scholars and arbiters, and Jewish sages, a man of letters, philosopher, and court physician.

He was born in Cordoba, Spain, but in 1160 when he was at the age of 25 he moved with his family to Fez, in Morocco. Following the persecution of the Jews in Fez Maimonides left the town and in 1165 arrived at the port of Acre in the Holy Land. He spent about five months in the country, touring the Land. He subsequently moved on to Egypt where he settled in Fostat, the old city of Cairo.

There Maimonides served as "Nagid" (governor) – head of the Jewish community in Egypt, and was appointed personal physician to the Sultan. It was in Egypt that Maimonides wrote his two major works: "Mishneh Torah" (compiled in 1180) and "Guide to the Perplexed" (compiled in 1190).

Maimonides died on December 13, 1204. Some years later his remains were brought from Egypt to Tiberias for burial. His grave is sought out by pilgrims to this day.

First page
of Maimonides' "Mishneh Torah",
printed in Soncino, 1490.

"...On the first night of the week, the third day of the month of Sivan, I came ashore in peace. I landed at Akko, saved from the Inquisition. We had arrived in the Land of Israel.

On that day, I vowed that I and my family would live lives of joy, happiness, feasting and giving charity to the poor, until the end of time..."

(Quote of Maimonides from a book by Rabbi Eliezer Azkari, 1588.)

Title page of Maimonides "Guide to the Perplexed", fourteenth century manuscript

As for your coming to my home, come with God's blessing! I am thrilled to hear it. I long for your company, and greatly look forward to seeing your pleasant countenance. In fact, my joy is greater than yours!..."

"I spend my time as follows: I dwell at Misr (Fostat, old Cairo) and the Sultan resides at al-Qahira (Cairo); these two places are two Sabbath days' journey distant from each other.

My duties to the Sultan are very heavy. I am obliged to visit him every day, early in the morning; and when he or any of his children, or any of the inmates of his harem, are indisposed, I dare not quit al-Qahira, but must stay during the greater part of the day in the palace. It also frequently happens that one or two royal officers fall sick, and I must attend to their healing.

Hence, as a rule, I repair to al-Qahira very early in the day, and even if nothing unusual happens, I do not return to Misr until the afternoon.

Then I am almost dying with hunger...I find the antechambers filled with people, both Jews and gentiles, nobles and common people, judges and bailiffs, friends and foes - a mixed multitude who await the time of my return.

I dismount from my animal, wash my hands, go forth to my patients, and entreat them to bear with me while I partake of some slight refreshment, the only meal I take in the twenty-four hours. Then I go forth to attend to my patients, and write prescriptions and directions for their various ailments. Patients go in and out until nightfall, and sometimes even, I solemnly assure you, until two hours or more in the night. I converse with and prescribe for them while lying down from sheer fatigue; and when night falls, I am so exhausted that I can scarcely speak.

In consequence of this, no Israelite can have any private interview with me, except on the Sabbath. On that day the whole congregation, or at least the majority of the members, come to me after the morning service, when I instruct them as to their proceedings during the whole week; we study together a little until noon, when they depart. Some of them return, and read with me after the afternoon service until evening prayers. In this manner I spend that day.

I have only told you a little of what you will see when you come, with God's help. When you finish your commentary for our brethren, copy it over, for when a man begins the performance of a commandment, he should complete it. Then, you will surely come with rejoicing!"

Illustrated title-page
of the thirteenth book of the "Mishneh Torah" by Maimonides, drawn by Nathan son of Simon the Levite, Cologne, 1296.

(From a letter of Maimonides to Rabbi Judah Ibn Tibbon, in which he thanks Ibn Tibbon for translating his treatise "Guide to the Perplexed" from Arabic to Hebrew, c. 1190.)

Maimonides

LANDMARKS OF THE ERA

Stamp of Maimonides

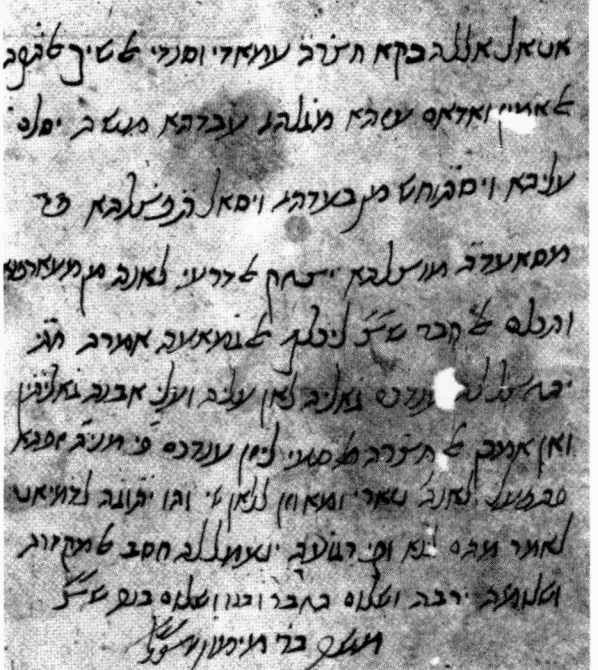

Maimonides handwriting and signature

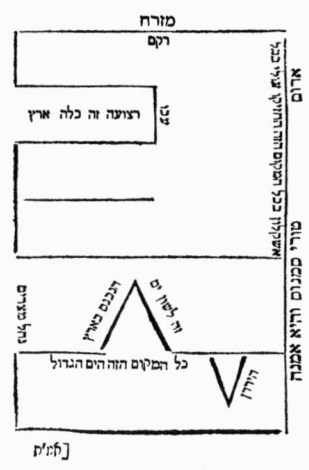

Plan of the Temple,
described by Maimonides in "Mishneh Torah",
thirteenth century manuscript

Design of the Land of Israel as drawn by Maimonides in answer to the question: "What is the western border of the Land of Israel?"

The answer of Maimonides: "The western border begins at Ashkelon. You will find this in what the Talmudic tract Gittin (pp. 6, 7) says about the Land of Israel. I shall sketch for you the Land of Israel and the place adjacent to it. This will make everything clear".

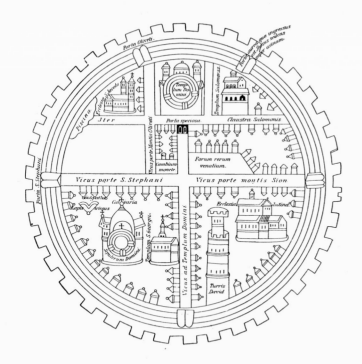

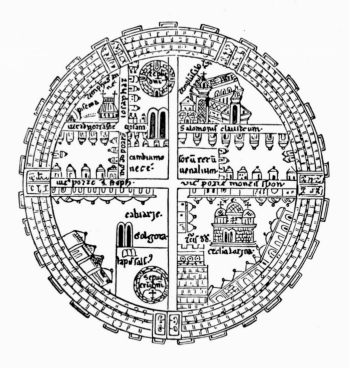

Section from a map of Jerusalem.
Crusader's manuscript, Germany, twelfth century.

Gold Coin, the eagle of King Frederick II.
Italy, 1231.

Section from a map of Jerusalem.
Crusader's manuscript, twelfth century.

The Seal of King Baldwin I, King of Jerusalem,
depicting the Tower of David, twelfth century.

The Seal of the Archibishop of Caesarea,
depicting the walls and the tower of the city, twelfth century.

1250-1492

SCHOLARS OF THE LAND

World map from "General Cosmography",
G. Le Testu, France 1555.

Sir John Mandeville

Portrait of Sir John Mandeville. From a fourteenth century German manuscript.

The little that is known of the life of Sir John Mandeville, English traveller of the 14th century, appears in the preface to his book written in 1360 upon his return from his voyages. In his book he describes himself as having set out on his travels in 1322, returning after some thirty-four years. His journeys brought him in 1336 to the Holy Land where he traversed the land, gathering detailed information about its towns and villages, their inhabitants and customs. Although Sir John Mandeville placed special emphasis on his descriptions of the Christian holy places, he also wrote about Jaffa, Caesarea, Atlit and Ashkelon.

His book accords a special place to Jerusalem. The city, its residents and churches are all portrayed with admiration and in great detail.

The book was considered a great success and during the centuries the manuscript was copied and reprinted in several editions. There were, however, conflicting opinions as to the authenticity of his descriptions, and it was said that they were compiled from various travel books.

"...The Holy Land, which men call the Land of Promise or of Behest, surpassing all other lands, is the most worthy land, most excellent, and lady and sovereign of all other lands..."

"...and that land He chose before all other lands, as the best and most worthy land, and the most virtuous land of all the world; for it is the heart and the middle of all the world; by witness of the philosopher, who saith thus "Virtus rerum in medio consistit", that is to say, the virtue of things is in the middle."

(From "Travels of Sir John Mandeville", 1360.)

Mount Sinai and St. Catherine's Monastery as depicted by Breuning, sixteenth century.

A nd forasmuch as for a long time past there was no general passage or voyage over the sea, and many men desiring to hear speak of the Holy Land, and have thereof great solace and comfort, I, John Mandeville, knight, albeit I be not worthy, who was born in England, in the town of Saint Albans, passed the sea in the year of our Lord Jesus Christ 1322, on the day of St. Michael; and hitherto have been a long time over the sea, and have seen and gone through many diverse lands, and many provinces, and kingdoms, and isles...

...And I shall devise you some part of things that are there, when time shall be as it may best come to my mind; and especially for them that will and are in purpose to visit the holy city of Jerusalem, and the holy places that are thereabout.

And I shall tell the way that they all hold thither; for I have oft-times passed and ridden the way, with good company of many lords: God be thanked!

And ye shall understand that I have put this book out of Latin into French, and translated it again out of French into English, that every man of my nation may understand it; and that lords and knights and other noble and worthy men that know Latin but little, and have been beyond the sea, may know and understand, if I err from defect of memory, and may redress it and amend it. For things passed out a long time from a man's mind or from his sight turn soon into forgetting: because a man's mind may not be comprehended or withheld, on account of the frailty of mankind..."

"...From Babylon to Mount Sinai, where St. Catherine lieth, you must pass by the desert of Arabia, by which Moses led the people of Israel; and then you pass the well which Moses made with his hand in the desert, when the people murmured because they found nothing to drink. And then you pass the well of Marah, of which the water was first bitter, but the Children of Israel put therein a tree, and anon the water was sweet and good to drink. And then you go by the desert to the vale of Elim, in which vale are twelve wells; and there are seventy-two palm-trees that bear the dates which Moses found with the children of Israel. And from that valley is but a good day's journey to Mount Sinai.

And those who will go by another way from Babylon go by the Red Sea, which is an arm of the ocean. There Moses passed with the Children of Israel across the sea all dry, when Pharaoh, king of Egypt, pursued him. That sea is about six miles broad. It is not redder than other seas; but in some places the gravel is red, and therefore they call it the Red Sea. That sea runs to the borders of Arabia and Palestine, its extent being more than four days. Then we go by desert to the vale of Elim, and thence to Mount Sinai. And you must know that by this desert no man may go on horseback, because there is neither meat for horses nor water to drink; wherefore they pass that desert with camels. For the camel finds always food in trees and on bushes, and it can abstain from drink two or three days, which no horse can do..."

Jerusalem.
From Sir John Mandeville's manuscript, fourteenth century.

Drawing from Sir John Mandeville's book.

John Mandeville

(From "Travels of Sir John Mandeville", 1360.)

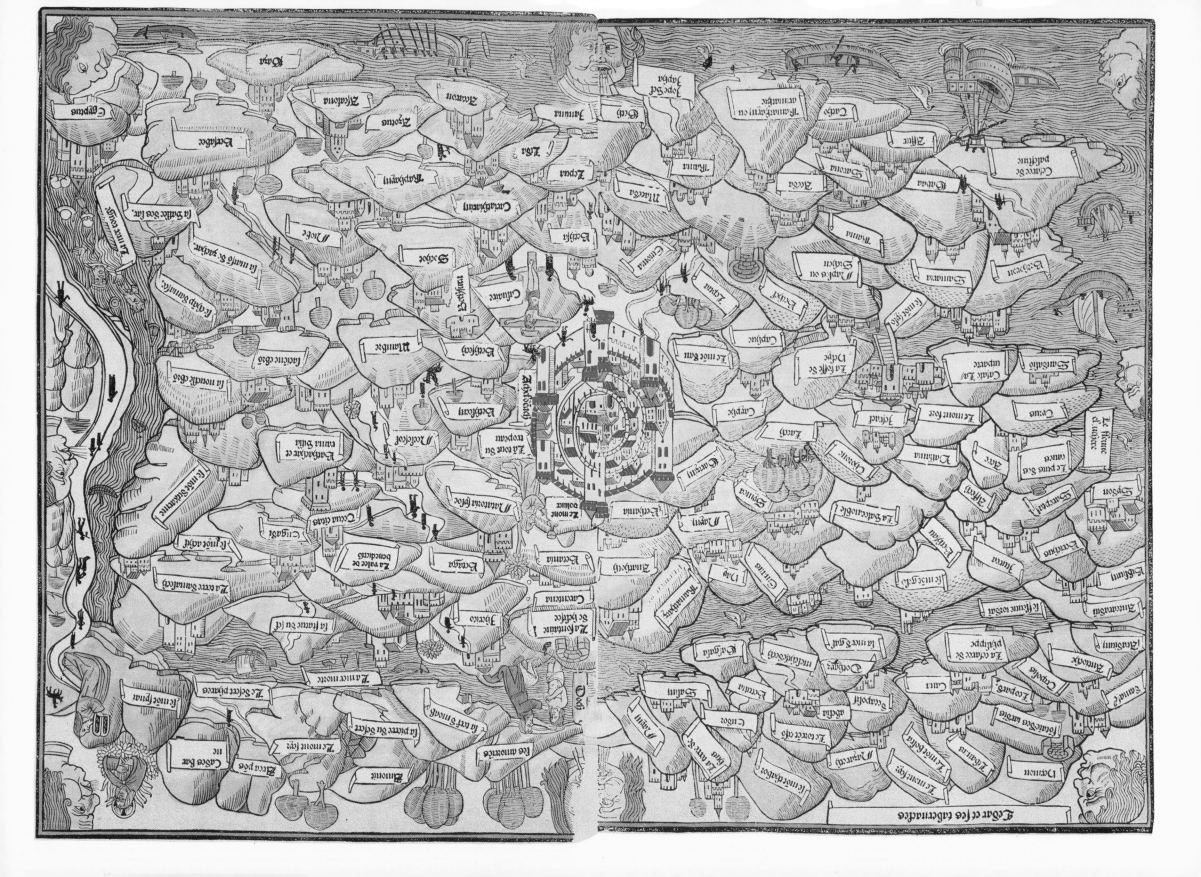

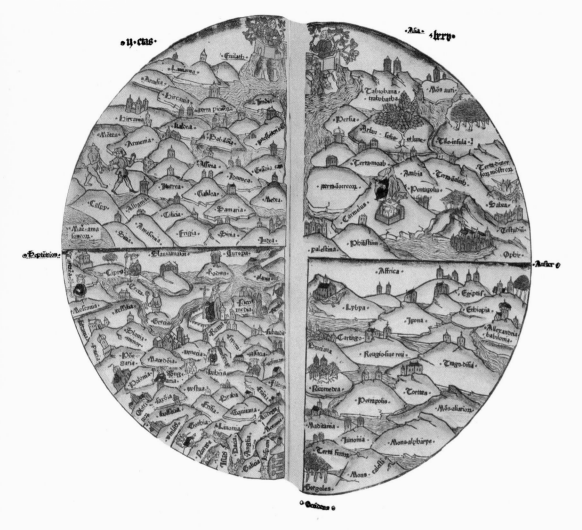

Map of the World – Anon.,
similar to the map of Lucas-Brandis de-Schass,
fifteenth century.

Map of Lucas Brandis de Schass
The Land of Israel

Map from the book of L.B. de Schass, "Rudimentum Novitiorum sive Chronicarum Historiarum Epitome" relating the history of the world, which appeared in Lubeck, Germany in 1475. The book is better known in its French edition, "La Mère des Hystoires", which first appeared in 1488.

The book contains several woodcuts, including two maps considered to be the first printed maps: a map of the world, and the map of the Land of Israel. Both maps face east. The latter offers a bird's eye view of the country, with Jerusalem at the centre.

At the northern border of the map are Sidon and Damascus, and at the southern end is the Red Sea. This was the first map to be made with movable type – some twenty years after the invention of the printing press by Johannes Gutenberg.

Jerusalem

Jerusalem stands out at the centre of the map. A wall with gates and towers surrounds it, and its main thoroughfare winds in a spiral path towards its centre. People are shown entering the gates of the city on foot, by cart, or riding a donkey. Surrounding the city are a number of holy sites: the Mount of Olives, Bethany, Calvary, the Gate of Mercy, and others.

The Coast in the Western Part of the Map

The Mediterranean Sea cuts across the width of the map, with the coastal cities of Israel – 'Akko, Caesarea, Jaffa, Ascalon (Ashqelon) and Gaza. In the lower right hand quarter are Egypt and the Red Sea. The mapmaker, as usual, equated this with the "Sea of Reeds" of the Hebrew Exodus from Egypt. Hence in the Red Sea we find the chariots and armies of Pharaoh which drowned there.

Northern Part of the Map

The Jordan River – The names "Jor" and "Dan" are marked in the northwest section of the map near Caesarea Philippi, i.e. Banias – flows across the width of the map, but the map chiefly shows the inland seas of the Land of Israel. On the banks we find the mountains of Gilead, the portrayal of a baptismal rite carried out by a priest, Bet-She'an and Jericho. Mount Sinai is drawn in the upper right part of the map, with Moses descending with the Tablets of the Law.

Eshtori HaParchi

Eshtori HaParchi (1280-1355) was the first man to carry out systematic research into the topography of the Holy Land. He was born in the south of France. There he acquired a broad general education, also studying medicine. He left France in 1306 and in 1313, after seven years of wandering reached the Holy Land and settled in Bet Shean where he established himself as a physician. He toured the country frequently, studying the names of its towns and villages and its antiquities. He also discovered the remnants of the ancient synagogues in Bet Shean and Hokkuk.

His book "Kaftor VaFerach", completed in 1322, mentions, inter alia, one hundred and eighty geographical sites named in the Scriptures, the Mishnah, and the Talmud. He was able to identify these locations in situ, and most facts as determined by him are deemed correct to this day. He furthermore effected comparisons between early coins, weights and measures, and those of his time, and furnished information and figures on various religions and sects in the Holy Land.

Title-page from "Kaftor VaFerach". Venice, 1549.

"By God's grace have I crossed the Land of Israel, most of its cities and states have I traversed. Among the scented hills I have found villages with spikenard. Of Bet She'an of Menashe where I sat to write this I chose to say the following: She that sits on many waters, stilled waters, a blessed, pleasant land, replete with joy, may she sprout forth like the Garden of God, and may she find the door of Eden."

(From his treatise, "Kaftor VaFerach", [5082], 1322.)

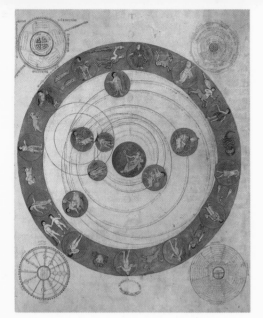

The Zodiac with the heavenly bodies.
From a fourteenth century French manuscript.

Floor mosaic from the Hamam (bath house).
Bet-She'an, sixth century.

The Zodiac.
From a French manuscript, fifteenth century.

Now I shall rise, says God. I shall be your shield." With God's help I shall reveal that which is hidden in this generation. As I said I would do in my introduction, I shall explain about the Land of Israel, its Biblical tribal boundaries and its cities, to those who are ignorant in these matters. This will help us so that when we pass through the Land of Israel, we will know just where miracle and wonders were performed, and we will be able there to give thanks to God for them.

I will call each place by both its Hebrew and Arabic names. That way, the traveler will be able to identify each place even though some of the Hebrew names have changed slightly. I enjoy searching for Biblical sites even more than searching for the stars of the Heaven, although nowadays definite similarities exist between the two.

That is, everyone knows that there are twelve constellations in the heavens, twenty-eight lunar camps and eight lunar patterns. Altogether then, there are forty-eight astronomical patterns, like the number of prophets. There are also seven planets, like the number of female prophets, and the heavenly sphere revolving round and round. Those planets pass over us constantly, yet few of us recognize them.

It is the same with the cities of the Land of Israel. People pass them to and fro, back and forth without knowing about them.

Therefore I have come, lowly and poor, to tell my brethren and my people what I have found out about this. It is not that I am wiser than those who have not dealt with this. I have only the advantage of having done the research and made the trip. I spent two years studying and researching in the Galilee, and another five years in the other tribal lands. During all that time, I did not desist for one moment from spying out the land. Blessed is He who helps the poor...

On Bet-She'an: I should not have to tell anyone that Bet-She'an is part of the Land of Israel. However, what choice do I have? Recently, individuals assumed to be experts have appeared, claiming that Bet-She'an is not part of the Land of Israel, but rather of the Diaspora. By saying this, they dissuade women and unlearned men from living there. Therefore, in order to raise the spirits of the downhearted, I write on this subject at length. My having been privileged to live there alone has not been my sole motivation for pursuing this. Rather, I wished to prevent our Biblical borders from being willfully and ignorantly diminished, lest this lead us to make light of the laws pertaining to them. Much later these individuals came here and retracted what they had said.

The reason I present Bet-She'an before you as a hub city, the source of instruction to all other places, is that it is only a half hour south of Tiberias, the center of the Land of Israel.

For this very reason I also sought out the advantages of Ramla, a city close to Lod, before discussing the borders of the Land. Ramla is yet another city which has been defamed."

Eshtori HaParchi

(From "Kaftor VaFerach", [5082], 1322.)

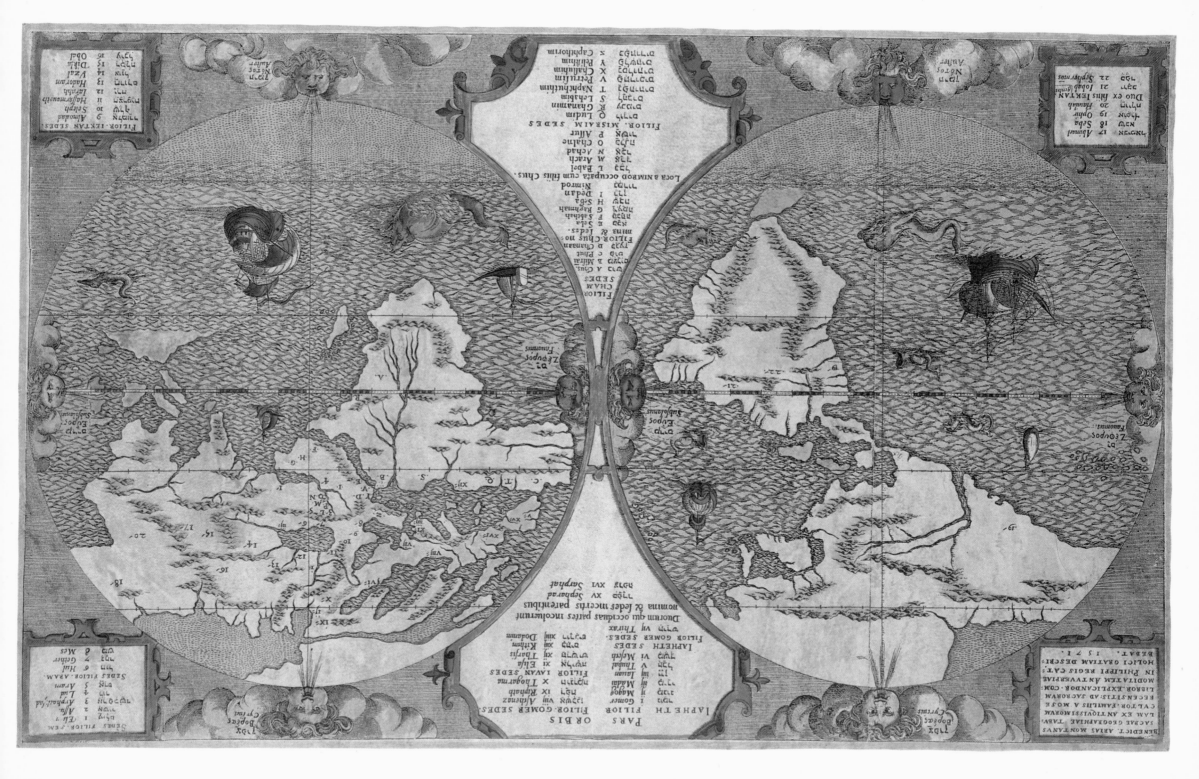

Page from the Polyglot Bible, 1569-1572, in 4 languages:
Hebrew, Aramaic, Greek and Latin in two versions.

Arias Montanus and the Polyglot Bible

Arias Montanus (1527-1598) was one of the most prominent men of letters of the sixteenth century. He lived and worked at the court of Philip II, King of Spain, devoting his life to researching the Hebrew language and the Bible. As a result he was accused by the Inquisition of harbouring a penchant for Judaism. Consequently there is a school of thought according to which he was a descendant of the Marranos, the Jews forcibly converted to Christianity.

Arias Montanus compiled the Polyglot (i.e. multi-lingual) Bible. This work, appearing in eight folio-sized volumes, was printed in the years 1569-72 at the printing press of Christoph Plantin in Antwerp, and represented the crowning glory of sixteenth century book-printing. It contained the Hebrew text of the Bible together with the translation of this text into four languages, constituting five parallel columns to a page. The Biblical world map before us appeared in volume 8 of the Polyglot Bible.

The Map

This Biblical world map shows how the nations of the world were dispersed after the Flood, and the inscriptions it contains are written in Hebrew and Latin. The names of the nations are taken from the "Chart of Nations" found in Genesis 10, and their markings (numerical or alphabetical) appear in all the continents of the earth.

On the frame of both hemispheres are figures of the four winds blowing in all directions, sending the ships of seafarers from one end of the world to the other. The continents of Europe, Asia, Africa and America are easily recognizable, and the tip of the unknown southern continent (Terra Australis Incognita), can be seen to the south-east.

PARS ORBIS

IAPHETH FILIOR.		FILIOR. GOMER SEDES.	
מומר	i Gomer	אשכנו	viii Aschenaz
מגוג	ii Magog	רפת	ix Riphath
מירי	iii Madai	חוגרמה	x Thogarma
יון	iiii Iauan	**FILIOR. IAVAN SEDES**	
תבל	v Thubal	אלישה	xi Elifa
משך	vi Mesech	תרשיש	xii Tharfis
IAPHETH SEDES		כתים	xiii Kittim
FILIOR GOMER SEDES.		רודנים	xiiii Dodanim
תירש	vii Thirax		

Inscription

(Upper middle inscription)

The inscriptions on all four sides of the map and in its centre contain the dedication by Arias Montanus to Philip II, who underwrote the costs of the Polyglot Bible – in his honour it is also called the Biblia Regia, i.e. the "Royal Bible" – as well as the table showing how the different peoples spread throughout the world. In the illustration before us is a chart of the Jefet dynasty, including the sons of Gomer, Jefet's son. Ashkenaz, the son of Gomer, is marked as the nation that settled in modern-day Germany, and Yavan, another son of Jefet, as the inhabitants of modern-day Greece.

Arnold von Harff

A pilgrim on his way to the Holy Land. From the von Harff treatise, 1860 edition.

Arnold von Harff was a relatively young pilgrim – only about 25 years of age – when he set out in 1496 to see the world. Such a journey, traveling through numerous countries, was made possible by the fact that his family was wealthy. He returned to his home town of Erft in Germany (for which he was named) in 1499.

Von Harff stayed in the Holy Land between the years 1498-1499, crossing the country from north to south. His manuscript was copied by hand many times over, and for several centuries served as a guide to German pilgrims visiting the Holy Land. It was first printed in 1860 in Cologne.

In his book von Harff provides detailed and interesting descriptions including the Hebrew alphabet and a short Hebrew-German dictionary of useful words he used in his travels such as tarngolez (Hebrew: tarnegolet, meaning hen); boissar (Hebrew: bassar' meaning meat, flesh); daegim (Hebrew: dagim, meaning fish).

"...And I should advise any pilgrim or peddler wishing to travel through heathen lands, to pay all travel duties, no matter what advice you receive from any Christian, Jew or Heathen (Moslem). These must be paid in every city and village. Furthermore, one must be wary of the temptations of strange women..."

(From "Travels of the Knight Arnold von Harff", 1499.)

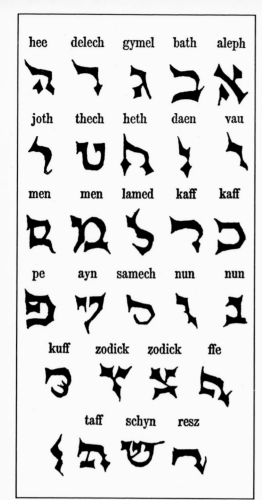

The Hebrew alphabet
and its vocalization
from the von Harff treatise, 1860 edition.

The alphabet characters shown: hee, delech, gymel, bath, aleph; joth, thech, heth, daen, vau; men, men, lamed, kaff, kaff; pe, ayn, samech, nun, nun; kuff, zodick, zodick, ffe; taff, schyn, resz.

The Temple Mount

Further along the way we reached Solomon's Temple, 160 paces away from the Tabernacle of Christ. By means of bribery, and after being promised total secrecy, I was brought by a Mameluk to this Temple, where neither Jews nor Christians are permitted to enter or even to approach. The Moslems claim that we are dogs, and that we are not fit – on pain of death – to walk in this holy shrine. This truly filled me with fear.

Solomon's Temple

This church, called "Porticus Solomonis", is much longer than Solomon's Temple. It has a pretty design, and is covered with a leaden roof. Inside there are forty-two marble pillars, and eight hundred candelabra burn constantly. Because the heathens (Moslems) greatly venerate this church, no Jew or Christian is allowed to come near.

In the Valley of Jehoshafat

Their cemetery stands before the gate in the vicinity of the Valley of Jehoshafat, and there they bury their dead. Therefore they guard the gate very strictly, lest Christians or Jews, worse in their eyes than dogs, trample their graves.

The Jews of Jerusalem and the Hebrew Tongue

In Jerusalem there are many Jews, among them Rabbis (sages), natives of Lombardia, who are experts on Christianity. There are also two Christian monks who converted to Judaism three years ago. I had many discussions with them and asked them many questions, but what was said is too lengthy to be put in writing. I also found three German Jews in Jerusalem, as well as some others in all the cities of the heathens (Moslems) and the Turks. The Hebrew language brought me to spend a great deal of time with them, and I learned to write the Hebrew alphabet. I remember a number of words from their language, and I have listed them on the following page.

A. Montegna:Detail of the City of Jerusalem, fifteenth century painting.

(From: "The treatise of Arnold von Harff", 1860 edition.)

Arnold von Harff

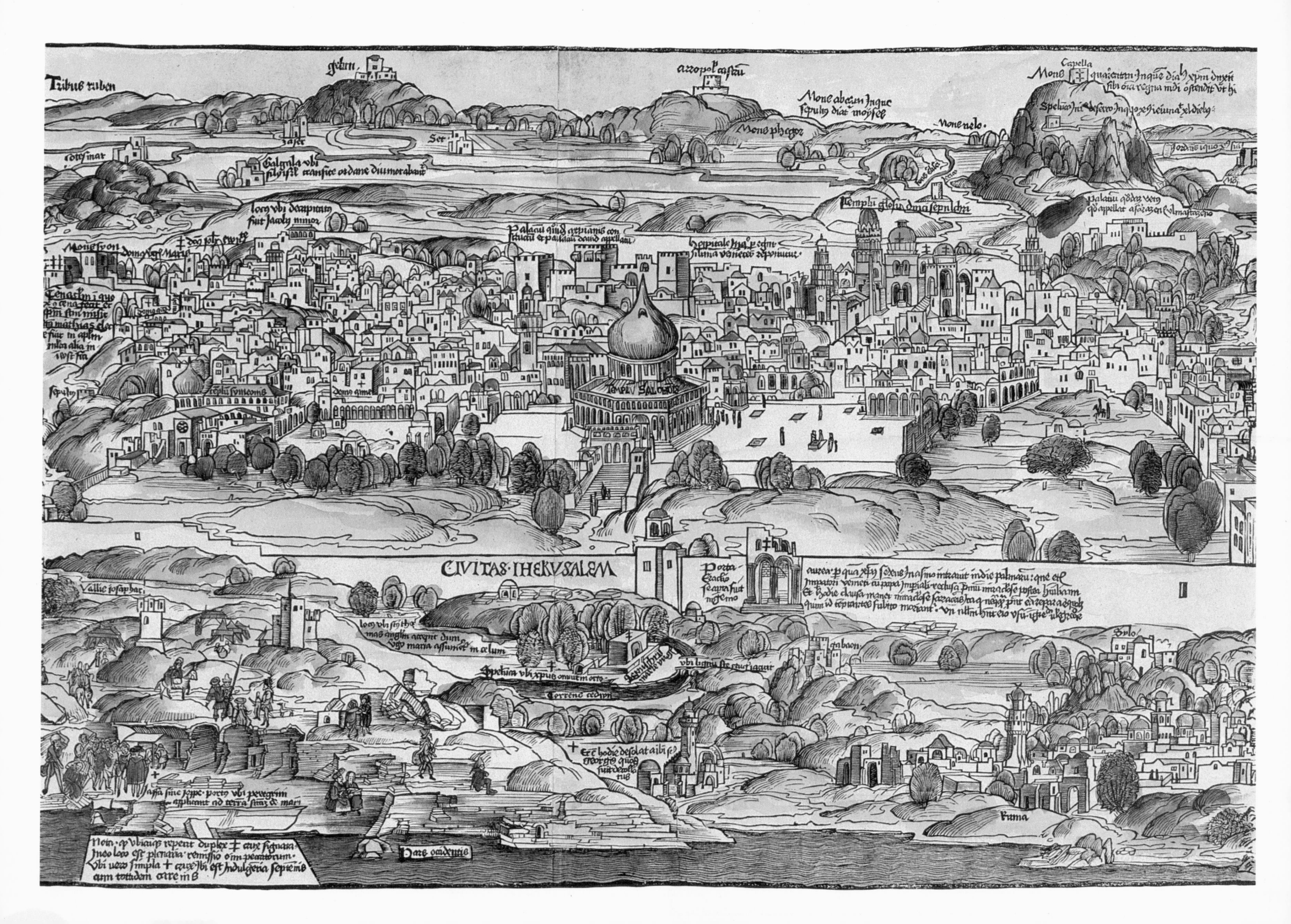

The Temple of Solomon in Jerusalem

Jaffa shore with ship and pilgrims

CIVITAS · IHERVSALEM

Bernhard von Breydenbach

The treatise by Bernhard von Breydenbach, "Peregrinatio in Terram Sanctam", "Travel to the Holy Land" first printed in Mainz, Germany in 1486, is the first detailed travelogue dealing with a journey to the Land of Israel. It has 148 pages, seven illustrations and a large map (some 130 cm. in length) of the Land of the Bible, the work of Erhard Reuwich, a Dutch artist who accompanied Bernhard.

For hundreds of years this was one of the most important and sought-after works on travels to the Land of Israel. It was translated into many languages and appeared in numerous editions. Bernhard von Breydenbach and Reuwich succeeded in faithfully portraying – both verbally and graphically – many sites in the Land of Israel.

A group of pilgrims headed by Bernhard, a deacon in Mainz Cathedral, set out from Venice in 1483, arriving in Jaffa on April 25. From Jaffa they left by caravan for Ramla, and from there they went on to Jerusalem, where they stayed a long time, visiting all the holy sites.

In addition, Bernhard carried out a daring trip to the Sinai Desert, to the Monastery of Santa Catharina at the foot of Mount Sinai. He moved on to the Red Sea, thence to Cairo, and from there he returned to Europe.

The Map

Before us is a section of the large map, showing Jerusalem in detail. While the entire map faces east, Jerusalem is depicted facing west, as it would appear when seen from the east.

At the centre - the Dome of the Rock with the inscription "Templum Salomonis" (Solomon's Temple). The structure to its left, with a smaller dome, is the al-'Aqsa Mosque, described by its Latin name, "Templum Symeonis". To the right of the Dome of the Rock, and northwest of it, stands the Church of the Holy Sepulchre ("Templum Gloriosum Domini Sepulchri"). Between these two shrines is a hospice for pilgrims. East of the eastern wall, in its southern (left) portion, is marked the Valley of Jehoshafat, part of the Valley of Kidron.

Near the inscription "Civitas Ihervsalem" (City of Jerusalem) in large letters, we find the "Porta Aurea" (Golden Gate), otherwise known as the "Gate of Mercy". South of Jerusalem, to the right, we note Rachel's Tomb and the city of Bethlehem. At the lower extremity we find the Mediterranean Sea and the shores of Jaffa, Ashqelon and other places.

Drawings by Erhard Reuwich
from the book by Bernhard von Breydenbach, 1486.

Syrian vine-growers on the hills of Jerusalem.

A couple in Jerusalem.

Turkish cavalry (Janissaries) on their way to the battlefield.

A group of Greek-Orthodox residents of Jerusalem.

The Hebrew letters and their pronunciation.

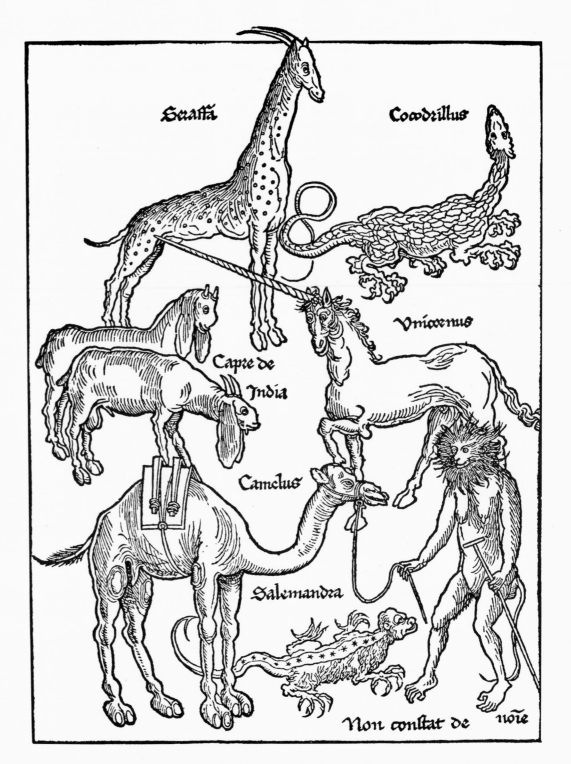

Animals in the Holy Land
as seen and drawn by Erhard Reuwich.

1492-1650

THE COURAGEOUS NAVIGATORS

PRVANA.

MAGALANICA.

ATLAS

ou

REPRESENTATION DU MONDE
VNIVERSEL ET DES PARTIES
D'ICELUI, FAICTE EN TABLES
ET DESCRIPTIONS TRES AMPLES
Tome second.

EDITIO

VLTIMA

Sumptibus & typis aeneis Henrici Hondij, Amsterodami 1638.

Title-page of the "Atlas" of Gerardus Mercator, published by Henricus Hondius.
Mercator was the first to use the term "Atlas" to denote a collection of maps.

Rabbi Ovadiah of Bertinoro

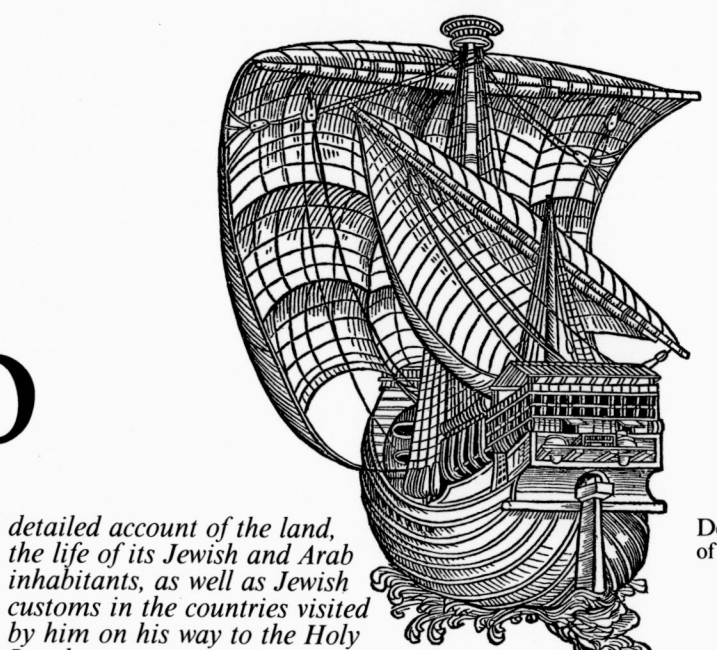

Design of a sailing ship of the fifteenth century.

Rabbi Ovadiah of Bertinoro (c.1450-1515) was named for the town of Bertinoro, in northern Italy, where his family originated. He is particularly well known for his interpretation of the Mishnah, first printed in Venice in 1548-1549.

In 1485 Rabbi Ovadiah left his residence in Castillo, Italy, and set out for the Holy Land, travelling for three years through Egypt and the Sinai desert, Gaza and Bethlehem, to Hebron. He reached Jerusalem in the spring of 1488. From there he dispatched a number of letters to his father, three of which have been preserved, and they give a detailed account of the land, the life of its Jewish and Arab inhabitants, as well as Jewish customs in the countries visited by him on his way to the Holy Land.

Rabbi Ovadiah stayed in Israel where he completed his interpretation of the Mishnah, later becoming head of a yeshiva in Jerusalem. He lived to a ripe old age, and was buried at the foot of the Mt. of Olives, near the Gihon spring.

"All the winds of the world come and blow through Jerusalem. It is said that every wind, before going to where it wishes to go, first comes to bow down to God at Jerusalem. Blessed is He who knows the truth."

(From a letter written in Jerusalem by Rabbi Ovadiah of Bertinoro to his father, (5248), 1488.)

A Moslem leader.
Sixteenth century design.

And from Jerusalem to Bethlehem it is about three parasangs, and the entire route is replete with vineyards and olive trees. The vineyards of this regions are rather like those of Romania, for the vines are short and stubby. A distance of three fourths of a parasang from Jerusalem there is a sort of ascent, and then you begin to descend. It was there that "the city of praise, the town of our rejoicing" came into view. There we tore our clothing as was our duty. A little ways further, the destroyed site of our Temple, our House of sanctity and splendor, became visible. We then tore our clothing a second time, for the Temple.

We came to the gates of Jerusalem and entered through them. It was the afternoon of the thirteenth day of the month of Nissan, 5248. On that day, "Our feet stood in your gates, O Jerusalem." A European Rabbi, raised in Italy, then came to greet us. His name was R. Jacob Di Colombano. He brought me to his house and I stayed with him all through Passover.

Most of Jerusalem is destroyed and desolate, and it goes without saying that it has no surrounding wall. The population, based on their own account, has around 4,000 householders.

Only seventy Jews remain today. They are poor and lack means of support. At the present time, whoever has enough money to support himself for the next year is considered rich. Numerous widows, old and lonely, from east and from west, bicker with each other, for there are seven women to every man.

Now there is peace and quiet in the land, for the Elders (community leaders appointed by the Sultan) feel regret over the evil they have done. They see that they are helpless, in fact more poor than they were at the start. When anyone wants to come and settle in the Land, they draw him close. They honour and exalt him, and offer abundant apologies for all the evil they did, saying they would only seek to do evil to someone who attempted to control them. Until now, I can only say that they have behaved well towards me, treating me fairly and leaving me in peace. Blessed is God every day!

As for the way the Arabs treat the Jews, the Jew can feel at home anywhere in this country. I traversed the length and breadth of the Land, and no one taunted or derided me. The Arabs treat the foreigner very mercifully, especially if he does not know their language. When they see a congregation of Jews together, they show no hatred at all.

In my opinion, if there was a man with political wisdom in this Land, he could be the prince and judge of both Arab and Jew. Among all the Jews of this region, not one has the wisdom to know how to get along with his fellow men".

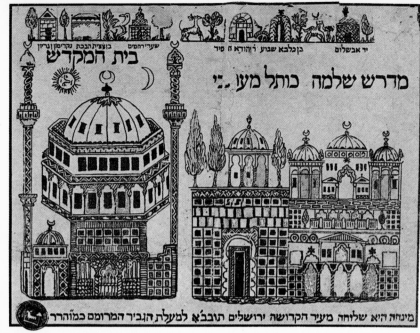

Holy Shrines in Jerusalem.
From a nineteenth century design.

Ovadiah of Bertinoro

(From a letter to his father, (5248), 1488.)

LANDMARKS OF THE ERA

Tycho Brahe's observatory. Copper engraving, seventh century.

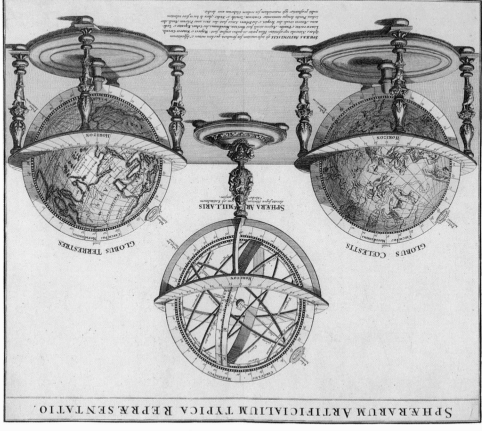

Armillary sphere
celestial and terrestrial globes,
eighteenth century.

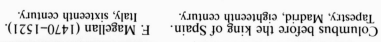

Columbus before the king of Spain.
Tapestry, Madrid, eighteenth century.

F. Magellan (1470–1521),
Italy, sixteenth century.

Marco Polo
Italy, sixteenth century.

Amerigo Vespucci on his mission to the New World.
Copper engraving, sixteenth century.

I. Stradanus: Cartographer with his tools in his study.
Copper engraving, sixteenth century.

Title page of the "Cosmography of the World",
London, 1682.

Rabbi Moses (Ben Mordecai) Basola

Elijah's cup, silver and gilt. Germany, seventeenth century.

Rabbi Moses Ben Mordecai Basola (1480-1560) was born in Pesaro, Italy. In 1521, at the age of 41, he set sail for the Holy Land, where he stayed for about eighteen months. He then returned to Ancona in Italy, where he became head of a yeshiva.

In a book by Rabbi Baruch of Livorno titled "In Praise of Jerusalem", and printed in 1785 (when Moses Basola's manuscript was first printed, though incomplete and inaccurate) Rabbi Basola describes his journey to the Holy Land, the towns visited by him and his impressions of the people, especially the Jewish communities. This travelogue contains many items of information on life in the country and its Jewish settlements in the 16th century. The travelogue has three appendices: a) Regulations and customs in Jerusalem. b) Investigations carried out by him regarding the Ten Tribes and the Sambation river. c) Practical instructions to pilgrims visiting the Holy Land.

In 1556 Rabbi Moses Basola returned to the Holy Land and settled in Safed where he later died in 1560 and where he was buried.

"... Four types of craftsmen do well in the Land of Israel: weavers, goldsmiths, cobblers and tanners.

Do not expect to find an apprenticeship in one of these areas. Also, do not expect to succeed as a shop keeper or a domestic servant. Therefore, unless you are independently wealthy, or possess one of the trades I have mentioned, do not leave Italy, lest you regret your decision and turn back..."

(From his book: "Journey of Rabbi Moses Ben Mordecai Basola", 1523.)

Title-page of the treatise "Kehillat Ya'akov", printed in Safed, 5338 (1578). This was the first Hebrew book printed in the Land of Israel.

On Tuesday before dawn we set out for Zefat. As the sun was rising, I was sitting on the pack camel, saying psalms and preparing to put on my phylacteries. Our three camels were tied one to the other, and mine was in the middle.

As we passed through a broad valley, a branch from a large walnut tree hit me in the face and knocked me over backwards to the ground. My head and spine collided so severely with the ground that I received a concussion and was paralysed. My breast bone was uncovered, and I was almost dead for a half hour. Several times I tried to say last confession, but I could not. Finally with great effort, I managed to say 'modeh ani' etc., thanking God for letting me live.

When I reached the city, no one took pity on me. Although I cried out for help, no one would pay me any attention. I wandered around, until God brought me to a widow who bandaged and treated me. Blessed is God whose kindness has not abandoned me. He has saved me from descending to the grave..."

"... Jerusalem is on one mountain, opposite the Mount of Olives. There is a narrow valley between them, the Valley of Jehoshaphat. I descended towards it, and I first came to a large pit, where a sort of cave is visible. It is said that in the future, on the day of Gog and Magog, the mouth of Hell will open there.

Further down the Mount of Olives, and on part of the incline towards Jerusalem, is the Jewish cemetery. Half a parasang further down are the waters of Shiloah, and many beautiful gardens derive their water source from there. The stream comes out of the Mount of Jerusalem, but its source is unknown. Some say it comes from the Temple. At the top one can see a building, a beautiful domed mausoleum. It is said that King Solomon used to make coins there.

Near it is a pit, called the Pit of Bigtan. It is said that Jewish girls threw themselves into it during the destruction of the Temple. There we find two beautiful caves, one made with crypts and the other with shelves in the wall. Further down is a broad tower with a sharp point. This is the Pillar of Absalom, mentioned in the book of Samuel. Above, near the top of the mountain, is the cave of Haggai the prophet.

There are caves of great length and circumference. The cave of Haggai the prophet is above. Further down are the graves of his students and some others. At the top of the Mount of Olives is a large house. There, within a beautiful citadel, is the marble grave of the prophetess Hulda. There as well one must pay an Arab guard an entrance fee of four drachma, and oil for lighting, as candles burn there at all times ..."

Title-page of "In Praise of Jerusalem" by Rabbi Baruch of Livorno, 1785. This book first related the travels of Rabbi Moses Basola.

Moses Basola

(From "The Journey of Rabbi Moses Ben Mordecai Basola", 1523.)

TERRA SANCTA
quae in Sacris
Terra Promissionis olim
PALESTINA

Amstelodami
ex officina Guiljelmi Blaeuw 1629

MARE MEDITERRANEUM

MARE SYRIACUM

MARE RUBRUM

Title-page from the "Atlas Novus"
by W.F. Blaeu, German edition, 1648.

Willem Janszoon Blaeuw (1571-1638)

For three generations during the sixteenth and seventeenth centuries the Blaeuw family were known in Amsterdam as producers and publishers of maps and atlases.

Willem Blaeuw, the founder, was born in 1571 in the city of Alkmaar north of Amsterdam. He studied science and astronomy under Ticho Brahe, the famous Danish astronomer, and later started out as a craftsman producing globes and scientific implements. Later on he was engaged in the engraving and publishing of maps. He published a comprehensive work on navigation and published the first maritime atlas, entitled "The Light of Navigation" ("Het Licht der Zeevaert"). For 200 years this work was an important aid to sailors, and was translated into many languages.

Blaeuw, too, published a world atlas, naming it "Theatrum Orbis Terrarum sive Atlas Novus" (Theater of the Terrestrial Sphere, or New Atlas"). The first two of twelve volumes planned for this atlas were published in 1635, and the work was completed by his sons, Jan and Cornelis, in 1655.

The Map

The map before us is taken from the first edition of the atlas (1635), but it had already been prepared in 1629, as can be seen from the inscription on the cartouche.

The coast extends from the Nile Delta at the map's western edge, to Tripoli in the east. On the map the Biblical boundaries of the tribes of Israel can be seen. The illustration in the bottom right-hand corner shows Moses holding the two tablets, and Aaron wearing the Ephod.

To the north and south we see two compass roses pointing north.

Sinai Desert: Near Mount Horeb (Sinai), the Children of Israel can be seen in their tribal encampments, surrounding the Tent of Meeting. Above Mount Sinai – clouds and fire: "And Mount Sinai was altogether on smoke, because the Lord descended upon it in fire: and the smoke thereof ascended as the smoke of a furnace, and the whole mount quaked greatly." (Exodus 19:18)

The map describes the Exodus from Egypt, starting in the city of Ramses in Goshen, and leading to the crossing of the Red Sea on dry land. The route through the desert from there until Gilgal is shown by a light-blue broken line. The forty-one desert encampments of the Children of Israel are illustrated by red tents. Cities are marked on the map with red buildings and towers. Sodom and Gomorrah are shown in the Dead Sea.

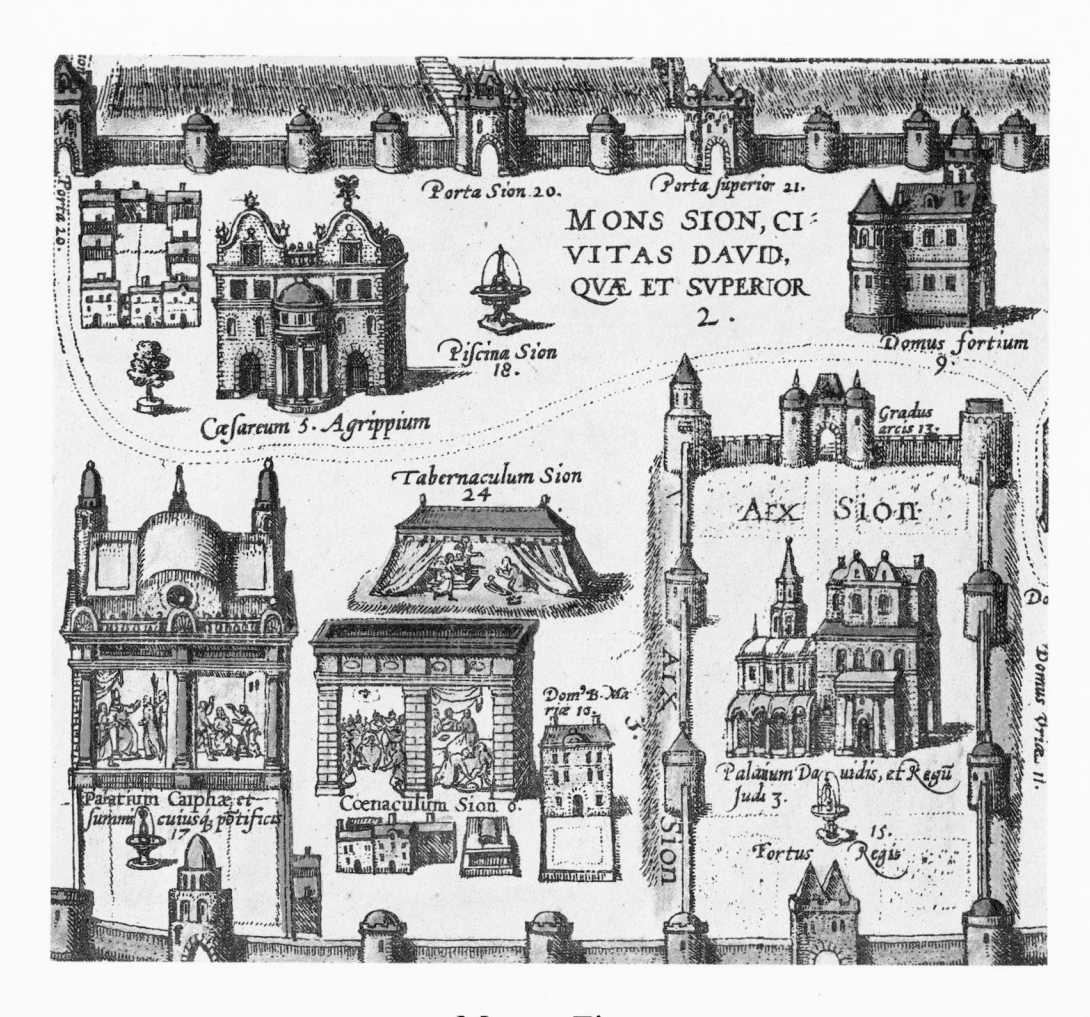

Mount Zion
with the palace of King David, *(detail)*.

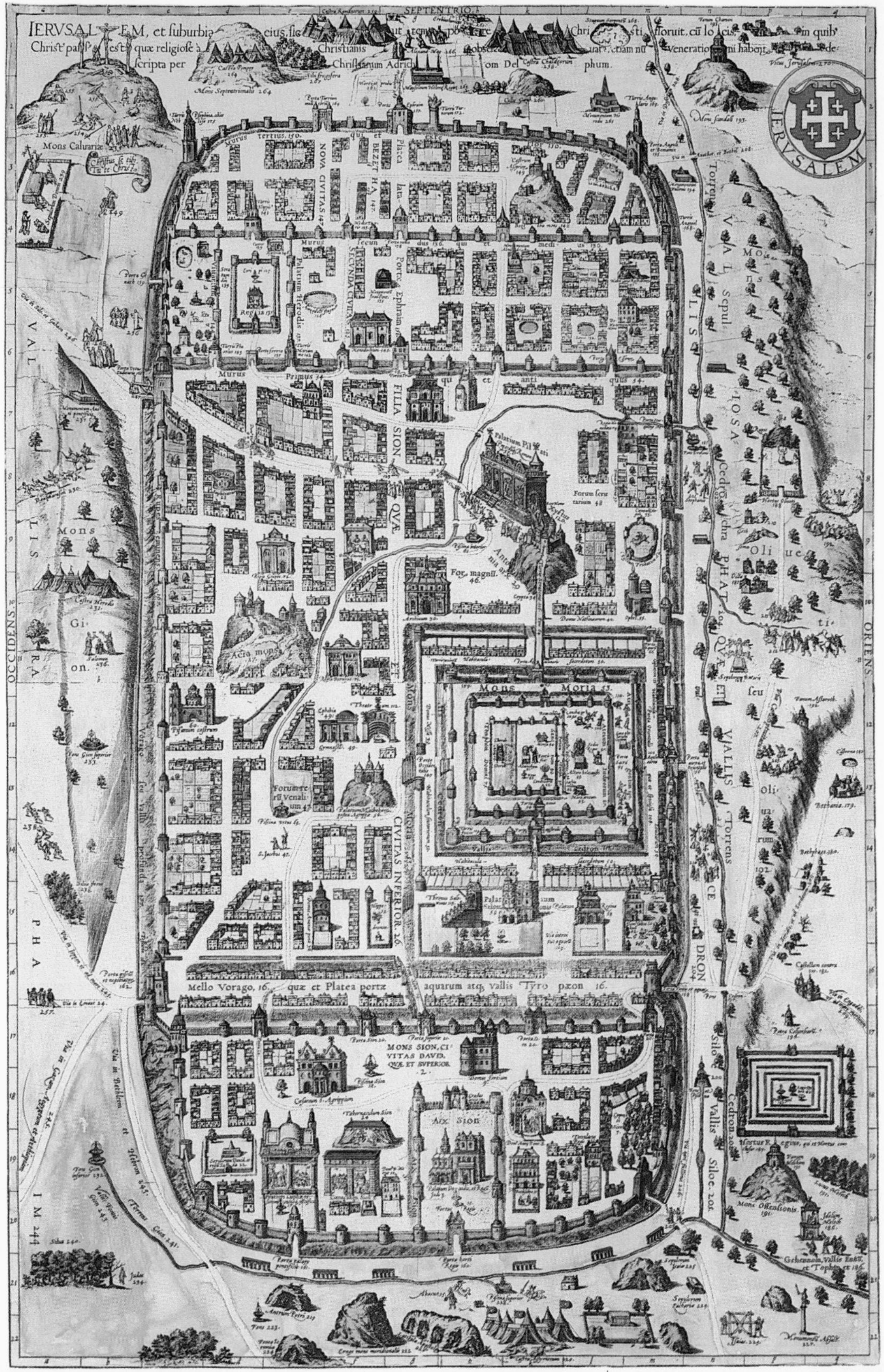

JERVSALEM, et suburbia eius, sic ... cum lo ... christ ... floruit, cum lo iei ... in quib
Christ passi ... est, quæ religiose ... descripta per ... om Del ... Chesæreum ... etiam nū ... Venerationi habent ... phum.

IERVSALEM

Mons Calvariae

NOVA CIVITAS

FILIA SION QVA

CIVITAS INFERIOR

MONS SION, CI-
VITAS DAVID,
QVÆ ET SVPERIOR
2.

Arx Sion

Mons Moria

VALLIS

Mons Gion.

OCCIDENS

ORIENS

VALLIS IOSA

Mons Oliueti

VALLIS CEDRON

Mello Vorago, 16. quæ et Plateæ portæ aquarum atq; vallis Tyro pzon 16.

Siloe Vallis

Mons Offensionis

Gehennom, Vallis Enar Tophet 127.

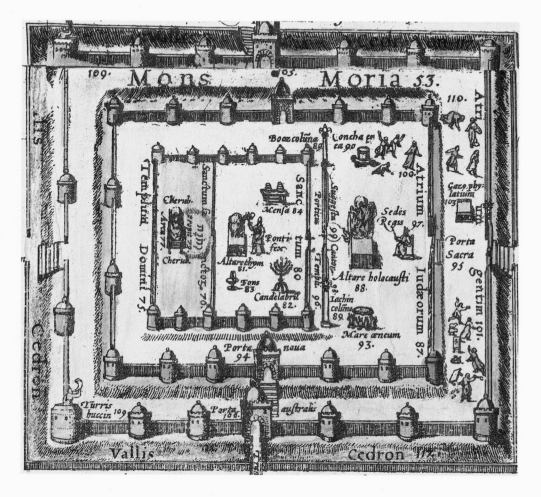

The Temple
with its walls, towers and gates, *(detail)*.

Christian Adrichom (1533-1588)

Christian Adrichom, a Dutch clergyman, was born in Delft in 1533, and acquired great expertise in the Holy Scriptures, as well as in all of the travel literature dealing with the Land of Israel. The map before us is an appendix to his book, "Theatrum Terrae Sanctae" (Theater of the Holy Land), which saw wide distribution in his day. The first edition was published at Cologne, Germany, in 1590. For two hundred years, this was the most important work concerning the geography of the Land of Israel. It included twelve maps of the tribal portions, a map of Israel, and the map of Jerusalem shown here.

The Map

The map before us combines the geographical, historical and architectural aspects of the city. Unlike most maps of Jerusalem that preceded it, this map faces north. For Jerusalem and its environs there are 270 reference points. They are described in detail, explained and numbered in the text of the book. The map includes the following details: major buildings of the city, such as the palace of Pontius Pilate (no. 57), from which the Via Dolorosa leads to Golgotha (no. 250). On the south-western side, the road leading to Bethlehem (no. 243) is marked. North of it we find a depiction of the anointing of King Solomon (236).

In the walls of Jerusalem we find the locations and names of the city gates. These as well are numbered and described in detail in the book. On the eastern side is the Valley of Jehoshaphat (no. 204). South of the city is Mount Zion, with the palace of King David (no. 2).

The Temple

There is a representation of the Temple, with its walls, towers and gates, on Mount Moriah. The inside of the Temple is depicted as well, showing the seven-armed candelabrum, the altar, and the table containing the shew bread. In the western part of the Temple lies the sanctuary, representing the Holy of Holies and the cherubs. As it is written:

"And he set the cherubims within the inner house: and they stretched forth the wings of the cherubims, so that the wing of the one touched the one wall, and the wing of the other cherub touched the other wall; and their wings touched one another in the midst of the house. And he overlaid the cherubims with gold."

(Kings I, 6:27-28).

LANDMARKS OF THE ERA
Maps of the Holy Land
from the sixteenth to the eighteenth centuries.

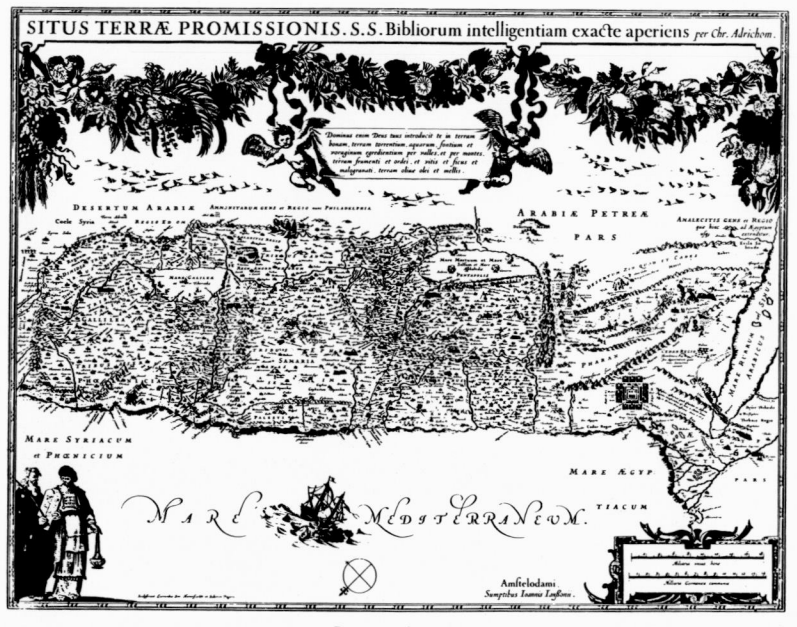

C. Adrichom
Map of the Holy Land published by J. Jansson.
Amsterdam, 1633.

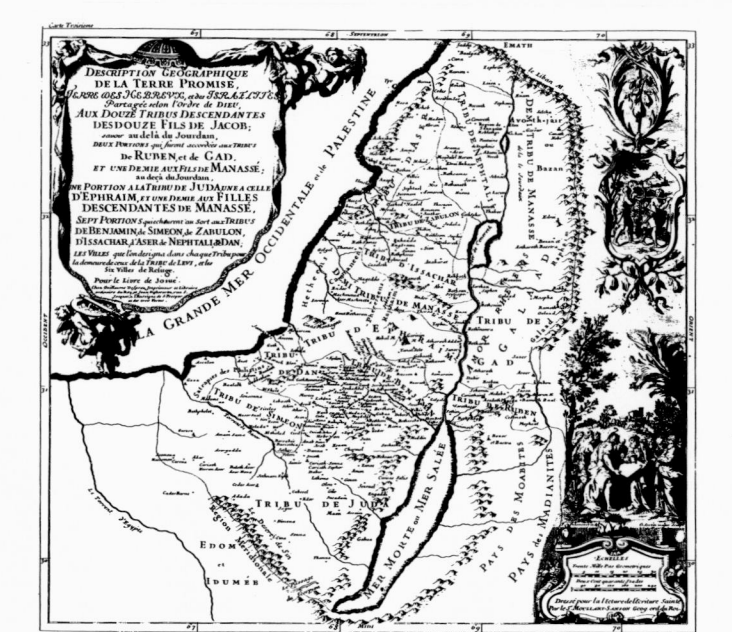

P. Moullart – Sanson
Map of the Holy Land divided into the tribes of Israel.
Paris, 1710.

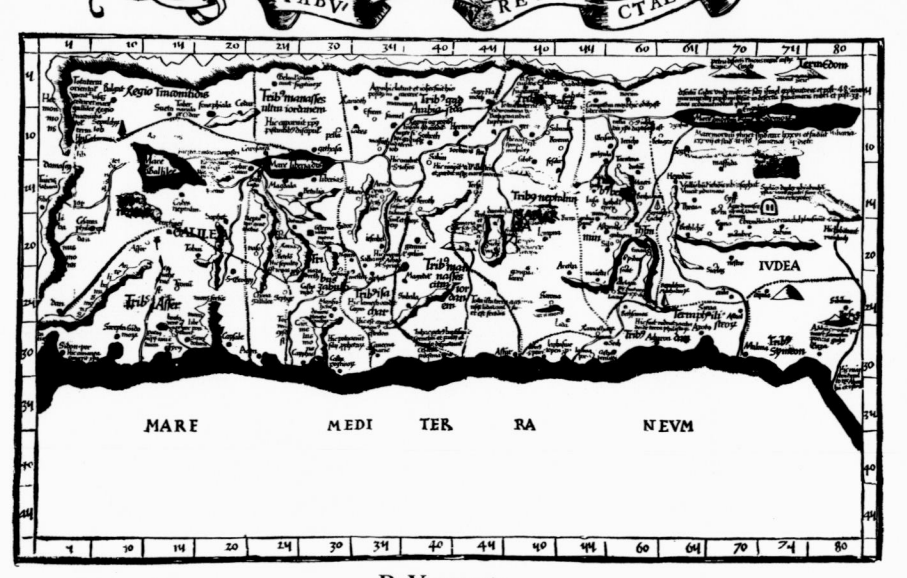

P. Vesconte
Map of the Holy Land in the book by C. Ptolemaios, Augsburg edition.
Germany 1535.

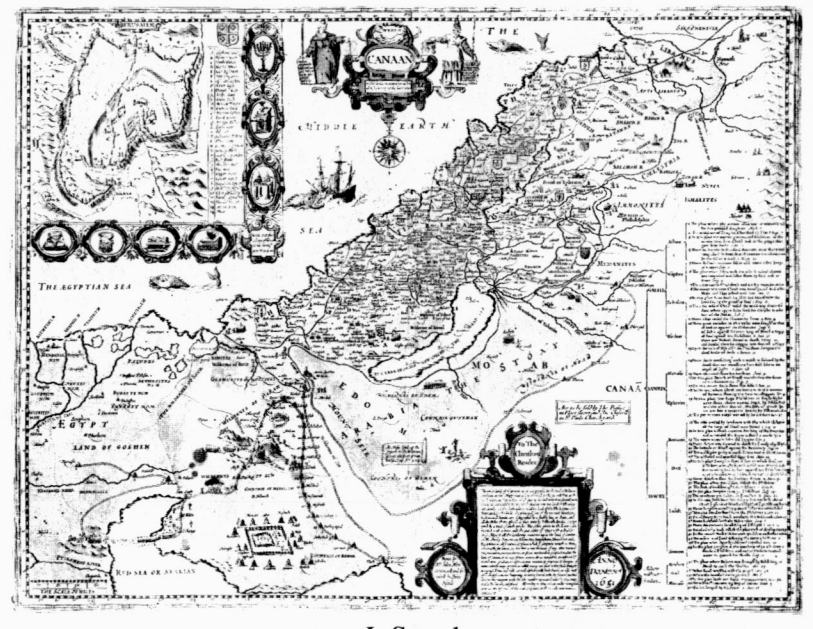

J. Speed
Map of the Holy Land, Egypt, and the city of Jerusalem.
London, 1651.

J.B. Homann
Map of the Tribes of Israel.
Nuremberg, 1700.

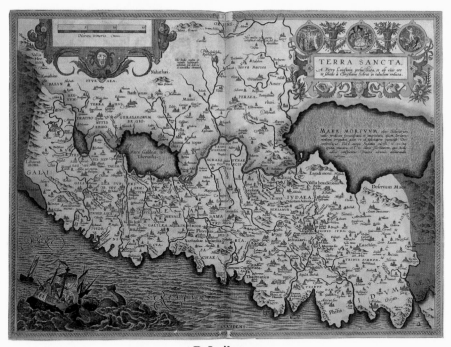

P. Laiksteen
Map of the Holy Land from the atlas by Abraham Ortelius.
Antwerp, 1586.

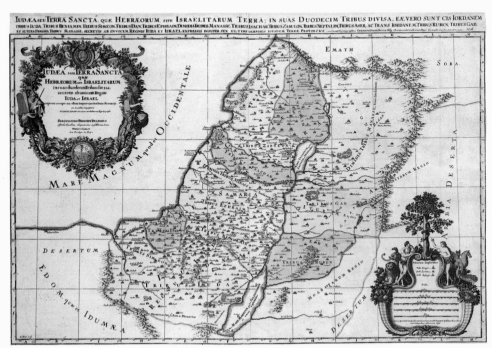

A. H. Jaillot – N. Sanson
Map of the Holy Land.
Paris, 1696.

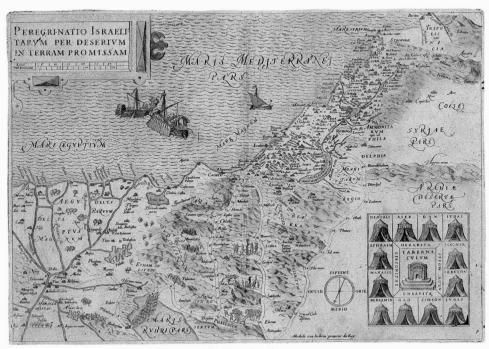

M. Van Lochom
Map of the Holy Land and the Exodus from Egypt.
Paris, 1660.

Eugène Roger

The sea of Genezareth (Tiberias). From T. Fuller map, 1650.

Eugene Roger was a Franciscan monk who arrived in the Holy Land in 1629 where he remained for several years, probably until 1634. He showed an interest in the various communities in the country, especially life in the Jewish community. His illustrated book, "The Holy Land", was published in 1664, serving as a highly detailed guide for tourists and pilgrims. The book starts with a description of his journey up to his arrival in the Holy Land, and then gives a detailed description of the various parts of the country, from north to south. Roger mentions, inter alia, Acre, Nazareth, Mt. Tabor, Tiberias, Haifa, the coastal plain, Ramla and Jerusalem and its environs. A description of the life and leaders of the Druse community also appears at the end of the book.

"... As a Rabbi told me, the Jews believe the Sea of Galilee was created from the broken sherds of the rock that Moses smote with his staff to bring forth water for the thirsty Jews in the desert. These rock sherds were kept by Miriam, the sister of Moses. She threw them down at this spot, and in one moment, created the body of water that we call the Sea of Galilee.

Jews, Christians, Arabs, and all peoples of the east admit that the water from this lake is of higher quality than that of any other lake or pond in the entire world..."

(From his book: "La Terre Sainte", 1664.)

Jew from the Holy Land,
depicted in E. Roger's book. Paris, 1664 edition.

Sixty paces from the Tomb of Zachariah is a tomb called the 'Pillar of Absalom'. This differs only slightly from that of Zachariah, for it is of the same size, and of one piece, except for a capital shaped like a flower vase that has been added to a pillar.

"It is believed that King David ordered this tomb made for his son Absalom. Nonetheless, Absalom was never buried there, for after he rebelled against his father, he died east of the river Jordan, and his corpse was covered with rocks in punishment for his rebellion. In memory of the curse of his Prophet-King father, all pilgrims who pass before the tomb, be they Christians, Jews, or Turks, throw a single stone into it. In this way, it has become half filled with stones. If not for this, it could have stood on an equal footing with the known wonders of the world..."

..."Not just Catholics honour and visit the Holy Land for religious reasons, but also non-believers, heretics, Jews and Moslems, as I have already mentioned. While I have seen several Dutch Calvinists, English Puritans, German Lutherans and Anabaptists come from the west, they were not as numerous as the rebels and heretics of the east, more than two thousand of whom arrive every year: Greeks, Armenians, Nestorians, Copts or Ethiopians. No day goes by without the arrival of Moslems from India, Yemen, Egypt, the Barbary coast, Greece, and various other countries.

Besides these, a large portion of those pilgrims going to prostrate themselves on Mohammed's grave pass through the Land. They wish to visit Jerusalem and the Temple Mount, to pray on the sacred Mount of Olives, in the Manger at Bethlehem, and in Hebron at the graves of Noah, Abraham, Isaac and Jacob. These sites are a matter of faith and piety for them, and they are permitted to go there to their heart's desire, without paying the ransoms and taxes exacted of Christians and Jews. They are also permitted to enter Jerusalem through whichever gate they wish.

Other pilgrims, Catholics, non-believers, heretics and Jews, all pay heavy taxes. The first time they enter Jerusalem they are only permitted to enter through Damascus Gate. A sentry-unit of Jannisaris is posted there to deal with these pilgrims. When one of them arrives, they ask him what sect he belongs to, and they hold him there until they inform the head of that sect of his presence. The sentry then approaches the Pasha with a request for entrance..."

LA TERRE
SAINTE,
OV
DESCRIPTION
TOPOGRAPHIQVE
tres-particuliere des saints Lieux,
& de la Terre de Promission.

Auec vn Traitté de quatorze Nations de differente Religion qui l'habitent, leurs mœurs, croyance, ceremonies, & police.

Vn Discours des principaux poincts de l'Alcoran, & ce que les Santons leur preschent dans les Mosquées.

L'HISTOIRE DE LA VIE ET MORT DE l'Emir Fechrreddin, Prince des Drus.

Et vne Relation veritable de Zaga-Christ Prince d'Ethyopie, aui mourut à Ruel prez Paris l'an 1638.

LE TOVT ENRICHY DE FIGVRES.
Par F. EVGENE ROGER Recollect, Missionnaire de Barbarie.

A PARIS,
Chez ANTOINE BERTIER, ruë Saint Iacques,
à l'Enseigne de la Fortune.

M. DC. LXIV.
Auec Approbation, & Priuilege.

Title-page of E. Roger's book "La Terre Sainte".

Eugène Roger

(From his book: "La Terre Sainte", Paris, 1664.)

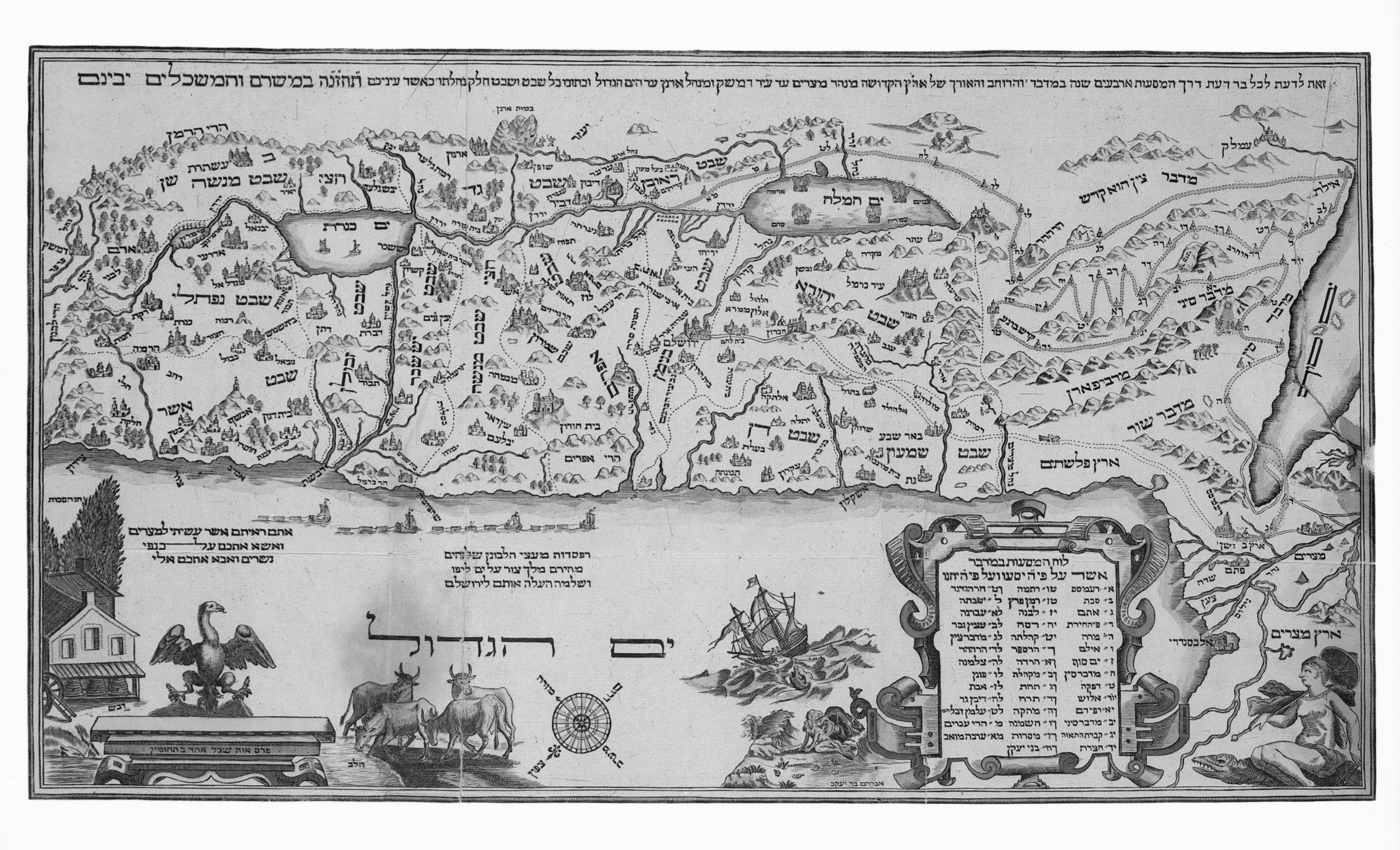

Title-page
of the Avraham Bar-Ya'akov Passover Haggadah,
including his Hebrew map, Amsterdam, 1695.

Avraham Bar-Ya'akov

Avraham Bar-Ya'akov, of German-Christian origin, converted to Judaism and lived in Amsterdam. He illustrated the Passover Haggadah with engravings, and produced fine engravings for other Hebrew works also, among them "Shenei Luchot HaBrit" (The Two Tablets of the Covenant), known by the acronym "ShLaH". This work was written by Avraham Halevi Horowitz, and printed in Amsterdam in 1695.

The Map

The map of the Land of Israel in Hebrew, by Avraham Bar-Ya'akov, was attached to the Passover Haggadah of 1695, published in Amsterdam. In this map we recognize the influence of Adrichom, whose map appeared in 1590. This influence is felt in style, in form, and in its facing east. It is even seen in the Hebrew names that appear on it, which mostly coincide with the Latin names on the map of Adrichom, although the map of Avraham Bar-Ya'akov is much smaller and contains fewer names. Two major sections to the map are apparent: the map itself, and the sea, with its various illustrations.

The Mediterranean Sea

This portion of the map is embellished and illustrated with Biblical verses. The construction of the Temple is recalled by means of several relevant verses, as well as by a drawing of seamen sailing down the coast bringing cedarwood from Tyre.

The Exodus from Egypt is recalled by the verse, "Ye have seen what I did unto the Egyptians, and how I bare you on eagles' wings, and brought you unto myself" (Exodus 19:4).

The Land of Israel, described as a land flowing with milk and honey, is illustrated with beehives (lower left-hand corner), and milch-cows.

The lower right-hand corner of the map bears a legend of the route of the Children of Israel in the desert, including a list of the forty-one stopping points. All points appear in the body of the map.

Route of the Children of Israel through the desert

The route is depicted by an orange line starting at the city of Ramses near the southern (right-hand) edge of the map, and ending at the Jordan crossing. The twelve stones, set down to signify the end of the journey after the crossing, are marked.

LANDMARKS OF THE ERA

N. Visscher
Title page of the "Atlas Minor"
(Small Atlas), Amsterdam, 1683.

A.H. Jaillot
Title page of the "Atlas Nouveau"
(New Atlas), Amsterdam, 1700.

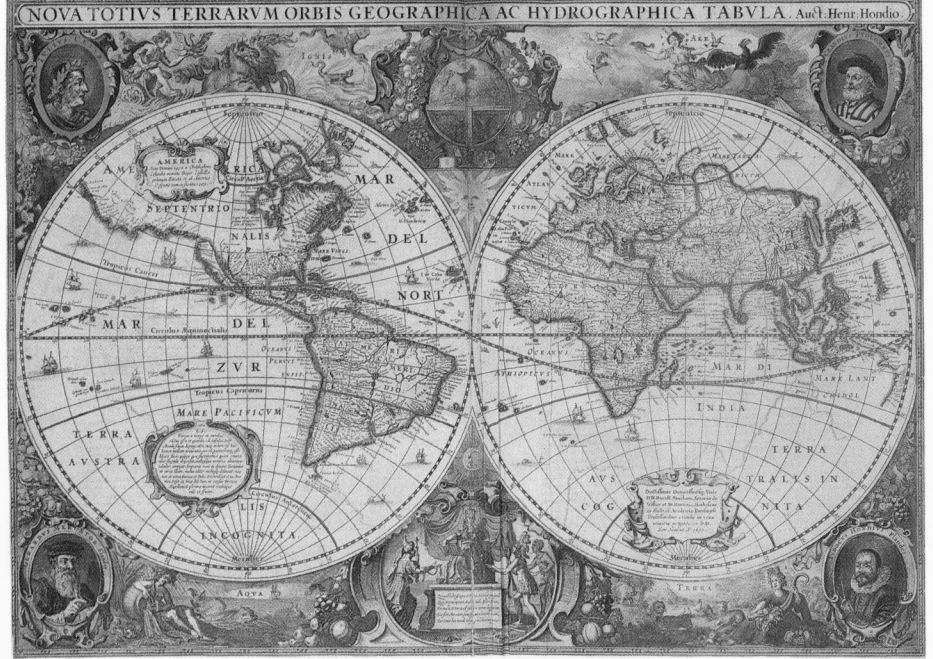

H. Hondius
World map from the Mercator atlas, 1636.

M. Seutter
Title page of the "Atlas Novus" (New Atlas). One of a series of atlases
published by the Seutter Family, between the years 1720-1741.

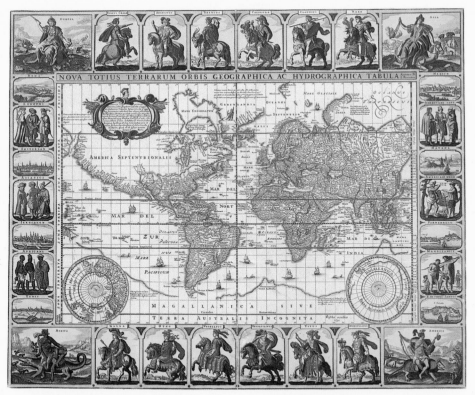

C.J. Visscher. World map. Amsterdam, 1652.

F. Hogenberg – G. Braun
Title page of the third volume
atlas "Theatrum Principarium Mundi", 1718.

F. Hogenberg – G. Braun
Title page of the fifth volume
atlas "Theatrum Principarium Mundi", 1718.

F. Hogenberg – G. Braun
Title page of the sixth volume
of the atlas "Theatrum Principarium Mundi", 1718.

1650-1750

TRAVELERS FROM AFAR

W. Van de Velde (The Younger):
The British Ship "Royal Sovereign" in a sea-battle, 1701.

Cornelis de Bruyn

Detail of Jerusalem.
From Braun – Hogenberg map,
copper-engraving, Germany, 1584.

Cornelis de Bruyn was a Dutch painter from the town of The Hague. During 1672-1683 he travelled to various countries, documenting and illustrating his travels, the scenery and the people he encountered, in a realistic and interesting manner. De Bruyn arrived in the Holy Land via Egypt in 1682.

Among the towns he visited were Jaffa, Ramla and Jerusalem, where he drew most of the Christian holy sites, *adding vivid descriptions of life in the Holy City. He also toured the northern part of the country, as far as Syria, later returning to Haifa and from there to Acre and Nazareth. His book, written in Dutch, was first printed in 1698 and contained 84 pages of engravings and 16 double pages of illustrations showing Jerusalem, Bethlehem, Alexandria and other towns.*

The book was translated into several languages.

"...On the 6th of November, three days after I started, I saw my picture of Jerusalem completed before me.

From my place on the summit of the Mount of Olives one is able to enjoy a beautiful view of the city, as the panorama is not disturbed by any intervening buildings. The most outstanding point is the big mosque, named after Solomon's Temple..."

(From "Travels of Cornelis de Bruyn", Delft, 1698.)

The Jewess,
depicted in C. De Bruyn's book, Delft, 1698.

The day after my return was a Sunday and I rested and did not go anywhere, but on the following day (Monday the 3rd of November 1682), I set out for Mount Olivet in order to sketch the city, but not to the place of Christ's lamentions, because all the others who had painted there before me always portrayed it from this direction. I, therefore, proceeded more to the south of the mount so as to draw my picture of the town as much as possible from the south-east. I was accompanied by two Franciscan padres and by the dragoman (interpreter), who were always on guard to prevent anyone from observing my doings. As a matter of precaution we had a basket filled with provisions and wine in readiness in order to impress casual passers-by with the idea that we were having a picnic. But despite this I was sometimes compelled to discontinue my work and wait for another day, because of the danger, as mentioned in my narrative on other Turkish places. The abbot of the monastery had implored me not to sketch the city as it might cause grievous unpleasantness to come upon the monastery if the Turks should notice me doing so.

But all in vain, for nothing in the world could have stopped me from carrying out my intention. I only promised him that I would take adequate measures to see that I was not caught and assured him that he could absolutely rely on my discretion, as I was fully aware where I stood and knew the Turks well enough.

...A beautifully decorated building, partly constructed of glazed tiles, which sparkle and shine in the sunlight, and specially the upper part of the structure, a dome covered with green and blue tiles, which gleams so brightly that it hurts the eyes. The roof of the Temple is entirely covered with lead, also its cupolas. At the top one sees a fairly big, gilt half-moon. The Temple square is very beautifully planted with trees."

(From his book: "Travels of Cornelis de Bruyn", Delft, 1698.)

Jerusalem.
Section from an illustration by Cornelis de Bruyn, Delft, 1698.

Cornelis de Bruyn

Henry Maundrell

Pilgrimage of a Franciscan Monk.

Henry Maundrell was an English clergyman and a member of the British Consulate in Aleppo, Syria. He set out to tour the Holy Land together with a number of English friends during Easter of 1697. The group visited various Christian holy sites and Maundrell held numerous conversations with Jews and Arabs during his travels. All these were described at length in the book. His descriptions are most detailed, including an historical background of the places visited. The book was first printed in 1714, and was translated into several languages. It was considered an interesting and useful travelogue for many years after its publication.

"...In the rockier regions where it is impossible to grow wheat, they cultivate vineyards and olive trees, which produce wine and olives in just those places where the most adverse conditions prevail..."

(From his book: "Journey from Aleppo to Jerusalem at Easter", 1697.)

Mount Tabor and surrounding area
from H. Maundrell's book, 1697.

Upon the former, the Samaritans, whose chief residence is here at Sychem, have a small temple or place of worship, to which they are still wont to repair at certain seasons, for perfomance of the rites of their religion. What these rites are, I could not certainly learn; but their religion consists in the adoration of a calf, and, as the Jews give out, seems to have more of spite than of truth in it..."

"...Our company halting a little while at Naplosa, I had an opportunity to go and visit the chief priest of the Samaritans, in order to discourse with him, about this and some other difficulties occurring in the Pentateuch, which were recommended to me to be inquired about, by the learned Monsieur Job Ludolphus, author of the Ethiopic History, when I visited him at Frankfurt, in my passage through Germany.

As for the difference between the Hebrew and Samaritan copy, before cited, the priest pretended the Jews had maliciously altered their text, out of odium to the Samaritans; putting for Gerizim Ebal, upon no other account, but only because the Samaritans worshipped on the former mountain, which they would have, for that reason, not to be the true place appointed by God for his worship and sacrifice. To confirm this, he pleaded that Ebal was the mountain of cursing, and in its own nature an unpleasant place; but on the contrary Gerizim was the mountain of blessing by God's own appointment, and also in itself fertile and delightful, from whence he inferred a probability that this latter must have been the true mountain, appointed for those religious festivals, and not (as the Jews have corruptly written it) Ebal. We observed that to be in some measure true which he pleaded concerning the nature of both mountains; for, though neither of the mountains has much to boast of as to their pleasantness, yet, as one passes between them, Gerizim seems to discover a somewhat more verdant fruitful aspect than Ebal. The reason of which may be, because, fronting towards the north, it is sheltered from the heat of the sun by its own shade; whereas, Ebal looking southward, and receiving the sun that comes directly upon it, must, by consequence, be rendered more scorched and unfruitful. The Samaritan priest could not say that any of those great stones which God directed Joshua to set up were now to be seen in Mount Gerizim, which, were they now extant, would determine the question clearly on his side.

I inquired of him next what sort of animal he thought those selavae might be, which the children of Israel were so long fed with in the wilderness. He answered they were a sort of fowl; and, by the description which he gave of them, I perceived he meant the same kind as our quails. I asked him what he thought of locusts, and whether the history might not be better accounted for, supposing them to be the winged creatures that fell so thick about the camp of Israel? But by his answer it appeared he had never heard of any such hypothesis..."

Mount Gerizim and Mount Ebal.
From maps by T. Assheton, 1818.

Henry Maundrell

(From "Journey from Aleppo to Jerusalem at Easter", 1697.)

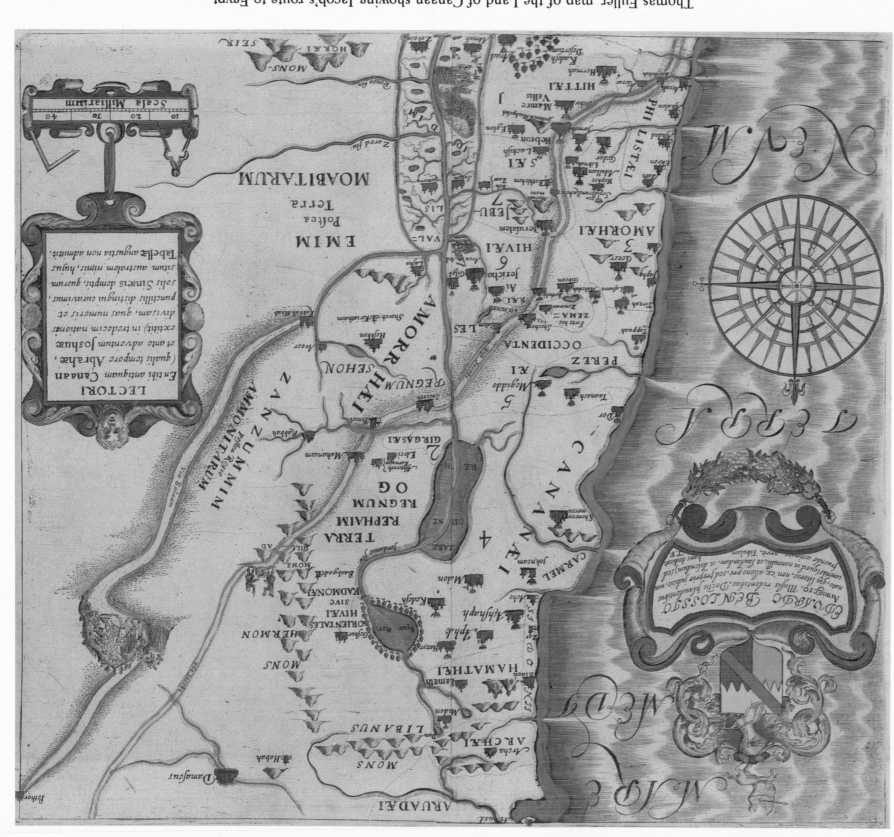

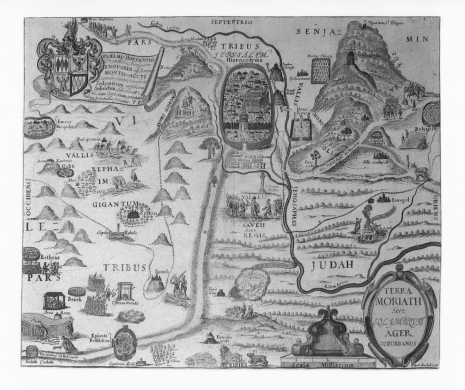

Thomas Fuller, map of the tribe of Judah.

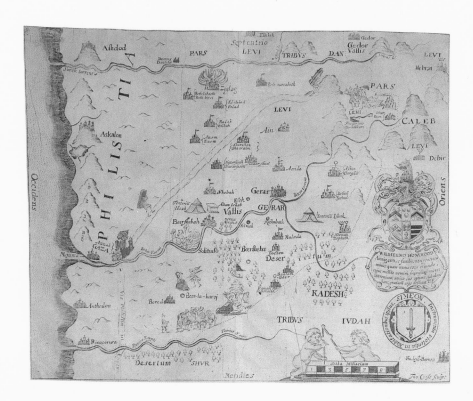

Thomas Fuller, map of the tribe of Simeon.

Thomas Fuller (1608-1661)

Thomas Fuller is well known for his book "A Pisgah-Sight of Palestine", published in 1650. The book is divided into sections, each dedicated to several patrons who contributed to the cost of publication. This practice eventually led to publication by enlisting subscriptions.

The above work, especially the 28 plates of engravings, was delayed, and carried out by several artists such as F. Clein, T. Cross, W. Marshall J. Goddard and R. Vaughan. Each map was dedicated to one of the donors, with an engraved coat-of-arms of the respective family.

The maps include: 12 maps of the tribes, 6 maps of the surrounding regions, 6 engravings of the Temple and its vessels, one large map of the Land of Israel, as well as maps of Egypt and Lebanon and two frontispieces.

The book was a great success, and for three centuries was considered the best and most beautiful collection on the Holy Land.

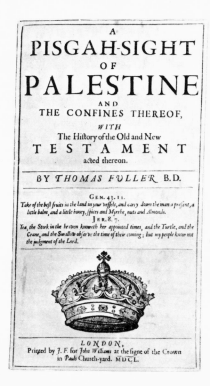

111

1799-1850

Napoleon at the Gates!

Napoleon's siege of Akko (Acre)
Drawing by Nicolas Charlet, who accompanied Napoleon on his travels. Lithography, 1799.

Napoleon Bonaparte

H. Wernet: Napoleon commanding the battle on horseback, 1809.

Napoleon Bonaparte (1769-1821), Emperor of France, was born in Corsica in 1769. From an early age he was educated in the military arts and proved to be an excellent student. During his military service Bonaparte earned rapid promotion and became known as a daring young officer. In 1796 he was appointed commander of the French army in Italy. Following his victories in the battlefield he was sent in 1798 at the head of a French army, to conquer Egypt en route to capturing India from the British. It was during this expedition that he invaded the Holy Land from the south-west, rapidly gaining control of the coastal strip up to Acre. There Napoleon and his army were stopped at the foot of the Acre battlements by the defenders within the city who were led by Jazzar Pasha and backed by a British naval force.

Despite Napoleon's two month-long siege of Acre starting March 19, 1799 he did not succeed in seizing the city and thus on May 22, 1799 decided on a retreat from Acre and from the Holy Land altogether. During his campaign Napoleon's army was struck down by plague. When he retreated he left behind hundreds of wounded and dying men. Napoleon returned to France, where he was hailed as a conquering hero. His defeat in Acre had but little influence on his further glorious career.

"...At the gates of Acre, my luck ran out..."

"...It wasn't a pleasant journey. It would have been better if I had stayed in Egypt. Today I would be the Emperor of the East..."

(From the book: "Journal de Sainte Hélène - 1815/1818", by A. Gourgaud.)

Appeal

F. Gerard: Napoleon the Emperor, 1810.

Bonaparte,

the Commander in Chief of the armies of the French Republic in Africa and Asia,

spoke thus to the legitimate heirs of the Land of Israel.

"Jews! Unique nation of the world! For thousands of years the world's tyrannical lust for conquest has succeeded in depriving you of your ancestral lands, but it has not eradicated your name, nor your national existence!

"Alert, impartial individuals have long been observing the fate of nations. Even if they are not blessed with the talents of seers, like Isaiah and Joel, they have still felt for a long time that the prophecies of those seers were correct. In their day these prophets saw the destruction of their kingdom and birthplace, and Isaiah said, 'Therefore the redeemed of the Lord shall return, and come with singing unto Zion, and everlasting joy shall be upon their head; they shall obtain gladness and joy; and sorrow and mourning shall flee away' (Isaiah 51:11).

"Awaken! Awaken, therefore, in joy, you exiled ones! A war such as there has never been in all of history is being waged now in self defence, by a nation whose enemies have plotted to plunder and divide among themselves the lands of its inheritance, through a stroke of the pen by their cabinets. This nation is presently avenging its wrath, and that of the most outcast nations, forgotten under the yoke of servitude. This revenge also avenges the two thousand year old shame that has been cast upon you.

"This war is taking place at a time that seems especially impropitious for your claims to be fulfilled, or even expressed. At present it is as though you are being forced to concede your claims totally. Yet, at this very moment, totally unexpectedly, we propose to return to you the inheritance of Israel!

"The young army, which Divine Providence has sent me here to command – this army, which is led by justice, and for whom victory is the constant companion, has made its centre at Jerusalem. In a number of days, it will move on to Damascus, leaving a region that will no longer threaten the city of David.

"Legitimate heirs of the Land of Israel!

"...Hurry! The moment has arrived to claim the return of your civil rights among the nations of the world, denied you for thousands of years. This moment may not recur for thousands of years more. You must claim for yourselves a national existence, as a state among states. You must claim your natural, unencroachable right to bow down before God, according to your faith, publicly and forever."

Napoleon Bonaparte

A.J. Gros: Napoleon visits plague victims in Jaffa, March 11,1799.

Napoleon Bonaparte

(From the book by Nathan Shor: "Napoleon in the Land of Israel".
Published by Am Oved, 1984.)

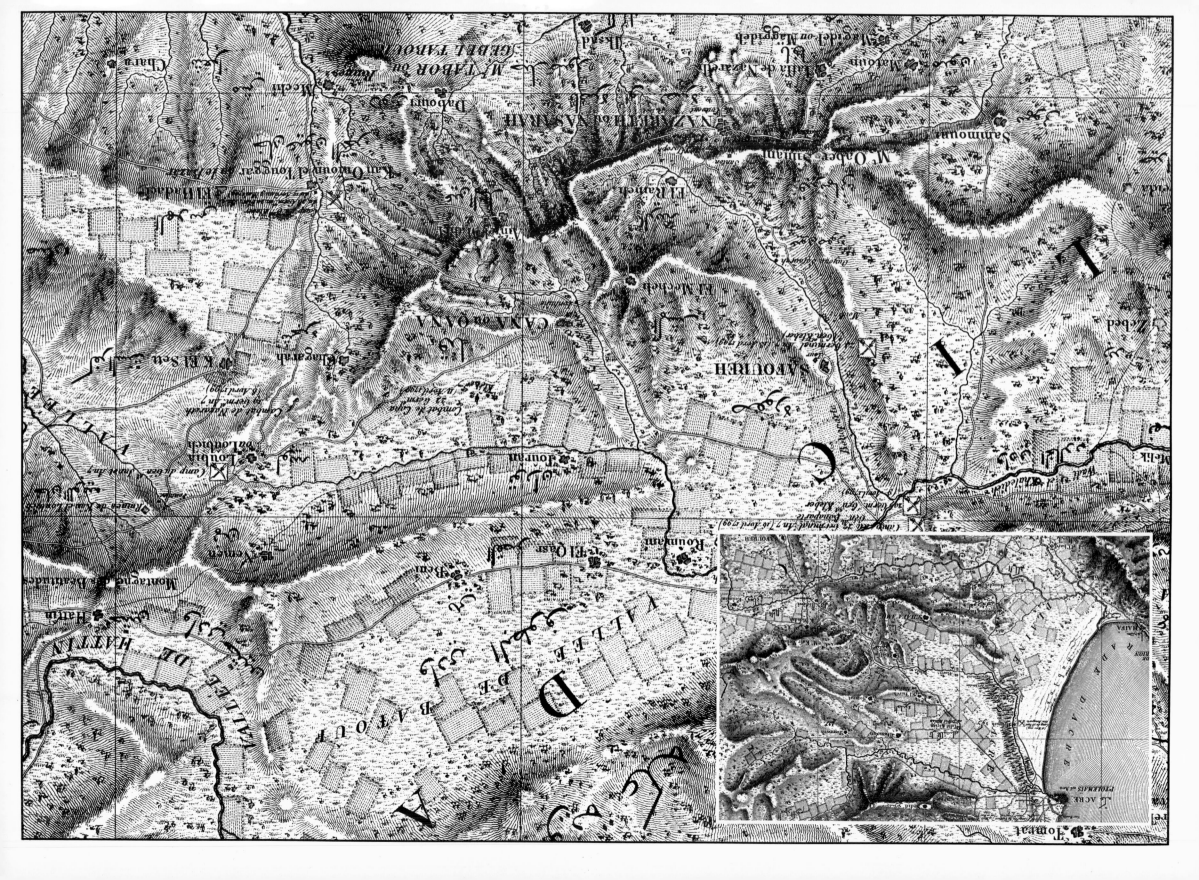

Napoleon's great (but temporary) victory in the Land of Israel.
The Battle of Tabor, April 16, 1799, in which the Turkish army was defeated,
painting by H.F. Phillippoteaux – L. Cognie.

Portrait of General Andoche Junot.

Portrait of General Kléber.

Map of Jacotin.

When Napoleon travelled to the Middle East, he was accompanied by the "Geographical Engineering Corps" under Pierre Jacotin. Jacotin's map, part of which is shown here, is one of the results of these travels. Some see it as the beginning of cartography of the Land of Israel in the new era. It was published as part of the comprehensive 18-volume study "Description of Egypt", under the name "Topographic Map of Egypt and of Several Parts of the Neighbouring Lands." In preparing the study the French used all the scientific means at the disposal of cartographers at that time: advances in mathematics and astronomy, sophisticated measuring devices, and modern printing techniques. Six out of forty-six of the map's sheets describe Palestine, but show only those regions through which the conquering French army passed.

The map depicts part of Napoleon's travels through the Land of Israel, the siege of Acre (the Biblical and present-day Akko), the attack, and the withdrawal routes of his army. It shows other aspects of the army's travels as well: camps and battlefields, with the names of the generals in charge, the route of advance and withdrawal of the forces, and the dates of battles. The names of settlements, regions and landscapes, mountains and rivers, are printed in two languages, French and Arabic.

The Battle of Tabor

The main battle between the French army and the Turkish forces took place in the Valley of Jezre'el, in the plain near 'Afula, and was called "the Battle of Tabor". At first, only a small French force was committed to carrying out the mission under the command of General Junot, but this officer found himself up against an enemy force that numbered four thousand cavalry and twenty thousand foot soldiers, and he doubted that he would be able to defeat such a force.

Napoleon, who at the time was near Acre, sent General Kléber with his forces on a night mission to aid General Junot. In a brilliant move he outflanked the Turkish forces. The army of the governor of Damascus and the great Turkish force, numbering over thirty thousand men, suffered a resounding defeat in this battle, waged on April 16, 1799. This victory enabled Napoleon to control the entire Galilee, but since he could not conquer Acre, it was impossible for him to realize his original plan, the conquest of Damascus. Napoleon was forced to withdraw and to return to Egypt, and from there to France.

The British Fleet in the battle of Acre, during the siege of Napoleon. Etching commemorating the fallen, 1803.

Bronze medal
commemorating Napoleon's Sanhedrin.
May 30, 1806.

DÉCRET IMPÉRIAL

Concernant les Juifs qui n'ont pas de nom de famille et de prénoms fixes.

A Bayonne, le 20 juillet 1808.

NAPOLEON, EMPEREUR DES FRANÇAIS, ROI D'ITALIE ET PROTECTEUR de la Confédération du Rhin;
Sur le rapport de notre Ministre de l'Intérieur;
Notre Conseil d'Etat entendu,
Nous avons décrété et décrétons ce qui suit:

ARTICLE PREMIER.

Ceux des sujets de notre Empire qui suivent le Culte hébraïque et qui, jusqu'à présent, n'ont pas eu de nom de famille et de prénoms fixes, seront tenus d'en adopter dans les trois mois de la publication de notre présent décret, et d'en faire la déclaration pardevant l'Officier de l'Etat civil de la commune où ils sont domiciliés.

Art. II.

Les Juifs étrangers qui viendraient habiter dans l'Empire, et qui seraient dans le cas prévu par l'article premier, seront tenus de remplir la même formalité dans les trois mois qui suivront leur entrée en France.

Art. III.

Ne seront point admis comme noms de famille aucun nom tiré de l'Ancien Testament, ni aucun nom de ville. Pourront être pris comme prénoms, ceux autorisés par la loi du 11 germinal an 11.

Art. IV.

Les Consistoires, en faisant le relevé des Juifs de leur communauté, seront tenus de vérifier et de faire connaître à l'autorité s'ils ont individuellement rempli les conditions prescrites par les articles précédens.
Ils seront également tenus de surveiller et de faire connaître à l'autorité ceux des Juifs de leur communauté qui auraient changé de nom sans s'être conformés aux dispositions de la susdite loi du 11 germinal an 11.

Art. V.

Seront exceptés des dispositions de notre présent décret, les Juifs de nos états, ou les Juifs étrangers qui viendraient s'y établir, lorsqu'ils auront des noms et prénoms connus et qu'ils ont constamment portés, encore que lesdits noms et prénoms soient tirés de l'Ancien Testament ou des villes qu'ils ont habitées.

Art. VI.

Les Juifs mentionnés à l'article précédent, et qui voudront conserver leurs noms et prénoms, seront néanmoins tenus d'en faire la déclaration, savoir: les Juifs de nos états, pardevant la mairie de la commune où ils sont domiciliés; et les juifs étrangers, pardevant celle où ils se proposeront de fixer leur domicile: le tout dans le délai porté en l'article premier.

Art. VII.

Les Juifs qui n'auraient pas rempli les formalités prescrites par le présent décret et dans les délais y portés, seront renvoyés du territoire de l'Empire. A l'égard de ceux qui, dans quelqu'acte public ou quelque obligation privée, auraient changé de noms arbitrairement et sans s'être conformés aux dispositions de la loi du 11 germinal an 11, ils seront punis conformément aux lois, et même comme faussaires, suivant l'exigence des cas.

Art. VIII.

Notre Grand-Juge Ministre de la Justice, et nos Ministres de l'Intérieur et des cultes, sont chargés, chacun en ce qui le concerne, de l'exécution du présent décret.

Signé NAPOLÉON.

Par l'Empereur:
Le Ministre Secrétaire d'Etat, *Signé* H.-B. MARET.
Pour copie conforme:
L'Auditeur au Conseil d'Etat Secrétaire général de la Préfecture,
F. HÉLY.

AVIS.

Les Personnes domiciliées dans le département de la Seine, qui se trouvent dans le cas des dispositions du Décret impérial ci-dessus rapporté, sont prévenues que les registres sur lesquels seront reçues les déclarations prescrites par ce décret sont ouverts dans toutes les Mairies dudit département, et que ces mêmes registres seront clos le 10 novembre prochain.

Paris, le 1er. septembre 1808.

Le Conseiller d'État Préfet du Département de la Seine, *Signé* FROCHOT.
Par le Conseiller d'Etat Préfet du Département de la Seine,
L'Auditeur au Conseil d'Etat, Secrétaire général de la Préfecture,
F. HÉLY.

De l'imprimerie de BALLARD, seul Imprimeur de la Préfecture du Département de la Seine, rue J.-J. Rousseau, n°. 8.

Napoleon's decree
ordering the Jews to adopt definitive family and first names, July 20, 1808.

Rabbi Yehoseph Schwarz

Portrait of R. Yehoseph Schwarz

Rabbi Yehoseph Schwarz (1804-1865) was born in Germany and came to the Holy Land in 1833, during the reign of Ibrahim, Pasha of Egypt.

As J.M. Lunz wrote in his foreword to Schwarz's book "Tevuot HaAretz" the craving for knowledge of the land of his fathers awoke in him when he was only 22. In 1829, before coming to the Holy Land, Yehoseph Schwarz had already published a map of the country in Hebrew and German. Upon reaching the Holy Land he settled in Jerusalem and set out to study the land in detail. He pub-lished several books on his research:"Te-vuot HaShemesh" (1843), "Tevuot HaAretz" (1845), "Pri Tevuah" (1861), "Pardes" (1861) and others.

In 1862 he added to his book "Pardes" fifty-nine answers on matters of Halakha, as well as a calendar and timetable of the daily sunrise.

Rabbi Yehoseph Schwarz died in Jerusalem in 1865. His tombstone still stands on the Mt. of Olives.

"More than four thousand times I sought to see the exact moment of sunrise. I climbed up on roofs, going sleepless in order to investigate the real truth... both during my sojourn overseas, and during my stay in the Holy Land..."

(From his book: "Tevuot HaShemesh", Jerusalem, [5603] 1843.)

"Dear brother,

Please forgive me if the style and language of this letter seem stilted to you, and if it does not contain what you wanted to find. I am in a rush to send it off to Beirut, from which it will travel to England by steamship. You surely are aware that a steamship has recently begun traveling back and forth between England and Beirut. By this route, letters from Germany arrive with more speed and certainty than when sent through Italy...

I hope you have already received my last letter, dated February 17 of this year, in which I described in detail the terrible earthquake of January 1, that struck the two Holy Cities of Zefat and Tiberias and environs. At that time, many thousands of people were killed. In this letter I will not touch upon that sad matter, the memory of which leaves me depressed even now. Most of the poor survivors were left without home or property. They have been received warmly in Jerusalem, and are being supported generously by the Jewish community here..."

"To commemorate the joyous Water Drawing Festival, special celebrations are held in the synagogue during the entire Succoth holidays. After evening prayer we hold a festive procession in the synagogue, and each celebrant holds a candle in his hands. During this joyous procession, a musical instrument called a "Temporicu" is played, similar to small drums.

In the recently built "Kehal Zion" synagogue, an exquisitely constructed device has been installed which sprays water up into the air during the festivities. This, together with the other customs of the holiday, is very impressive. On Shemini Atzeret, as well as on the night following (the night of Simchat Torah where you live), all the Torah scrolls are removed from the ark, and we dance in a circle with them.

...If someone is married during the week, a beautiful canopy stands in the synagogue on the following Sabbath, and the bridegroom sits under it with his best man. When the bridegroom is called up to read from the Torah, his grooms accompany him when he ascends and descends. When he completes the recitation of the Torah blessing following the reading, the cantor sings the seven verses starting with, 'Abraham was old', and continuing until '...take a wife unto my son from thence' (Genesis 24: 1-7). He reads first the Hebrew, and then the Aramaic translation, of each. During this song, the "shamash" (synagogue beadle) circulates with a bottle full of rose water, sprinkling a little into the hand of each of those present. This is carried out with great decorum..."

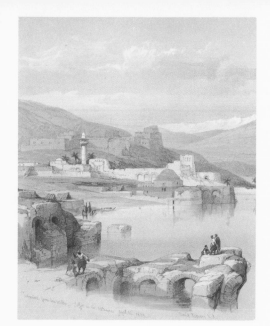

Tiberias,
Lithography by David Roberts, 1839.

Drawings by R. Yehoseph Schwarz

Jews disembarking at Jaffa.
Lithograhy by David Roberts, 1839.

Drawing by R. Yehoseph Schwarz

Yehoseph Schwarz

(From a letter sent to his brother from Jerusalem [5597], 1837.)

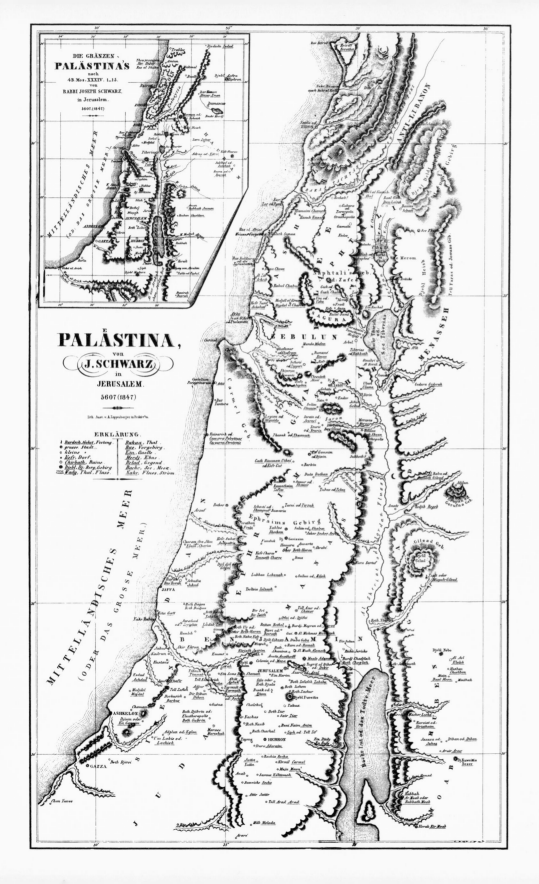

DIE GRÄNZEN
PALÄSTINA'S
nach
4B.Mos.XXXIV. 1.15.
von
RABBI JOSEPH SCHWARZ.
in Jerusalem.
5607.(1847)

PALÄSTINA,
von
J. SCHWARZ
in
JERUSALEM.
5607 (1847)

Lith. Anst. v. A.Oppenheimer in Frankf. M.

ERKLÄRUNG.

DIE GRÄNZEN
PALÄSTINA'S
nach
4 B. Mos. XXXIV. 1=15.
von

Rabbi Yehoseph Schwarz (1804-1865)

R. Yehoseph Schwarz was born in Germany in 1804 and immigrated to Palestine in 1833 during the reign of Ibrahim Pasha. He settled in Jerusalem, and in 1845 completed his treatise "Tevuot Ha'Aretz". This dealt with the borders of the Land of Israel, its geography, tribal divisions, Biblical names and places, Jerusalem and the Temple Mount.

In his introduction to this work, he described the method of his research in the following words: "I shall now write what I saw with my own eyes. I climbed mountains, descended into valleys, searching well. Some things I examined repeatedly, listening to truthful people, in order to arrive at the absolute truth."

Yehoseph Schwarz continued in the path of Eshtori HaParchi (see page 75), for he studied the ancient topography of the Land of Israel. In a letter to his brother in Germany he told of his research into the history of the Land, its population, customs and scenery.

The Map

The map of the Land of Israel drawn by R. Yehoseph Schwarz was published in Germany in 1829. It appeared in two languages, Hebrew and German, and was printed in three editions.

In Jerusalem, R. Yehoseph Schwarz wrote two additional books, "Pri Tevuah" and "Pardes", further to his interpretations of the Bible based on his research into the Land of Israel. These books were published in Jerusalem, 1861. Schwarz died in 1865, and was buried on the Mount of Olives in Jerusalem.

The Palestine Exploration Fund (P.E.F.)

The first topographic map of the Holy Land was made by the surveyors and cartographers of the British Palestine Exploration Fund. This very detailed map, surveyed between 1870 and 1877, was published on a scale of 1:63,360 (one inch to the mile) in London in 1880. It consisted of twenty-six sheets.

The British surveying staff was headed by Lieutenants C.R. Condor and H. H. Kitchener (who for a while was the British Secretary of War). Although they enjoyed the assistance and protection of the Turkish authorities, surveyors of the P.E.F. were repeatedly attacked by Arabs. In 1880 the large map was published in England, accompanied by three volumes ("The Survey of Western Palestine") describing the population, scenery and archaeology of the Holy Land, as well as the "Name List", a volume containing the name origins of all places mentioned in the map.

123

1897-1948

"...If you will, it is no fairy tale..."

Dr. Theodor Herzl on a balcony overlooking the Rhine,
Basel, Switzerland.

Dr. Theodor Herzl
(Benjamin Ze'ev)

Dr. Theodor Herzl
with his three children in his study.
Vienna, 1900.

Dr. Theodor (Benjamin Ze'ev) Herzl (1860-1904), founder of political Zionism and of the World Zionist Organization, was born in Budapest, Hungary. There he began his studies, until his family moved to Vienna in 1878. He completed his law studies in Vienna, later obtaining his doctorate in 1884. Soon afterward he decided to devote himself to writing.

As a journalist for the "Neue Freie Presse" in Paris, he was assigned to report on the Dreyfus Affair. The manifestations of anti-Semitism he encountered both in the courtroom and outside it had an enormous impact on him, heavily influencing his attitude toward the Jewish issue. From then on he saw the solution to the Jewish problem in the establishment of an independent Jewish State. He began to seek assistance and support for his idea, negotiated with the Rothschilds, hoping for their financial support, but was unsuccessful. He then decided to present his ideas to the public through his book "The Jewish State"

which was published in 1896 and subsequently reprinted in 80 editions and 18 languages. He tried again in a later book of his: "Altneuland", published in 1902.

In 1897 he organized the first Jewish Congress in Basel, where he was elected chairman of the World Zionist Organization. Herzl visited the Holy Land in 1898 with the intention to persuade the major leaders of that time – the rulers of the Ottoman Empire, Britain and Germany – to help him realize his plan to establish a Jewish State in the Holy Land. His attempts proved unsuccessful.

Herzl died in 1904, aged 44. In his will he asked to be buried next to his parents in Vienna, "until such time as a Jewish State is established, when my remains will be taken there...".

As bequeathed, Herzl's remains were brought to Israel in 1949 and were interred on Mt. Herzl in Jerusalem.

> "...At Basel I established the Jewish State. Were I to say this today, everyone would deride me. Perhaps in five years, and certainly in fifty, it will be universally accepted...."

(From his diary, 1897.)

Jerusalem, October 29.

"...The end of my address to the Kaiser: This is a homeland of ideas, not the definitive possession of one nation or another. To the degree that men ascend culturally they will recognize that which is general and that which is shared in these ideas. Thus, the earthly Jerusalem, with its walls etched in fate, has become a symbol, holy to all men of culture.

The Kaiser of peace has heroically come to the eternal city. We, the Jews, greet his Majesty at this exalted moment, and our prayer, from the depths of our heart, is that the days of peace and justice will come to all men on earth, and to our nation as well..."

October 29.

"...I must also note what has happened during the last three days since we left Rishon LeZion. We left it in the morning. A half hour from there is the Jewish village Wadi al- Hanin (Nes Ziona) where the entire population greeted us. Children sang, an old man offered me bread and salt and wine produced by his soil. I had to visit almost every farmer's home.

"...In Rehovot there was an even greater demonstration. All the residents waited for me, ordered in rows, and the children sang. These poor people gave me a royal welcome.

In the intense heat, we traveled back to Jaffa, and I arrived there exhausted..."

"At 9 o'clock a great movement along the way foretold the approach of the Kaiser and his entourage. The road was full with a motley crowd of Arab beggars, women, children and horsemen. Turkish riders galloped back and forth, unbridled, with threatening rifles and with eyes casting fear all around. Then the first horsemen of the Kaiser became visible, and there, in a group with a few nobles – the Kaiser himself.

"I gave the signal to the children's choir of Mikveh Yisrael to sing the anthem, "Heil Dir im Siegerkranz". I stood by one of the ploughs and removed my tropical hat. The Kaiser recognized me from afar. He moved a little and turned his horse towards me. I walked two steps towards him. He leaned on the horse's neck, and stretched out his hand to me. I approached him and gave him my hand, standing there with bared head. He smiled and his commanding eyes sparkled at me: 'Is everything all right'?

'Fine, your majesty. Thank you! I have been investigating the Land. How has your majesty's trip been so far?' The Kaiser winked hard at me and said: 'Very hot! But this land has a future.'

'Right now it is still sick,' I said. 'It needs water, much water!' he said from his seat. 'Yes, your majesty. Canals on a large scale.' "Then he repeated, 'It is the land of the future!'..."

Dr. Theodor Herzl
on his way to the synagogue. Basel, 1897.

Dr. Theodor Herzl with companions
in front of the house where he stayed in Mamillah street. Jerusalem, 1898.

Dr. Theodor Herzl
in "tourist garb" on donkey-back,
visiting a Turkish port.

Theodor Herzl

(From Dr. Theodor Herzl's diary, 1897.)

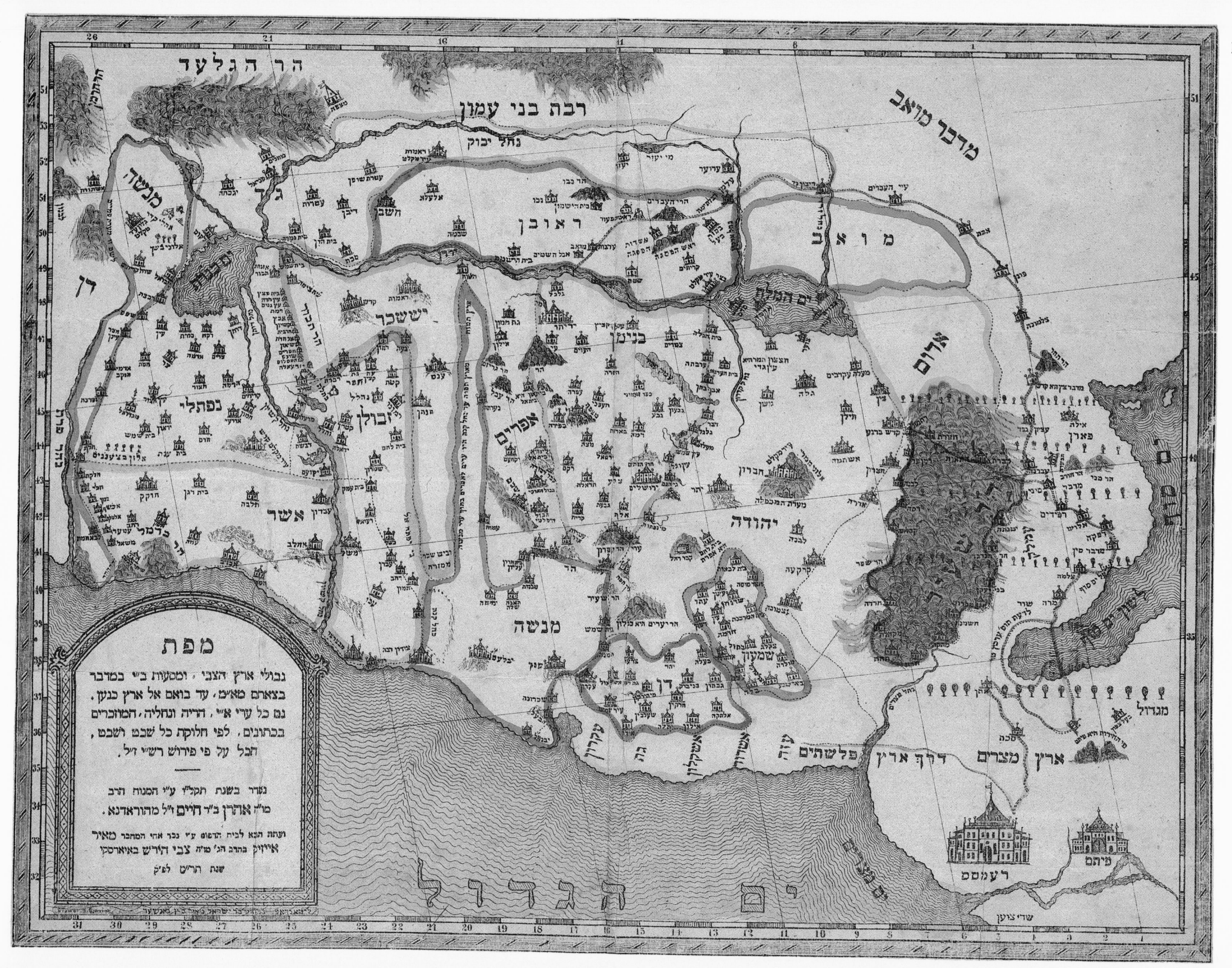

Begießen der Orangen   Petach-Tikwah
No. 18   השקאת פרדס   פתח תקוה

1.

Gedera

2.

Kolonie Sichron-Jacob

זכרון יעקב

3.

1. Petah-Tikva,-Irrigating an orchard, 1890.

2. Gedera, 1890.

3. Zikhron Ya'akov on the slopes
of Mount Carmel, 1901.

4. Rosh-Pinah in Galilee, 1910.

4.

Map of Rabbi Aharon Bar Haim

This map of the Land of Israel, by Rabbi Aharon Bar Haim, first appeared in his "Guidebook" published in Horodna in 1836. A newer edition was printed in Warsaw in 1879 under the title "Map of the Boundaries of the Holy Land". The map was published by Rabbi Bar Haim's grandson Zvi Hirsch.

This map shows the Tribes of Israel established in their respective lands, as well as the route taken by the Children of Israel on their exodus from Egypt – from Ramses to the Jordan River. The wayside stations where they encamped are marded by small illustrations. The lower right-hand corner of the map shows the towns of Pithom and Ramses, indicated by drawings of palaces.

Petah-Tikvah

Today a city in Israel's coastal plain. Founded in 1878 by Jerusalem Jewish residents as the first Jewish village in the country, Petach Tikva became known as "Mother of the Moshavot".

The settlement was aided by the famous Rothschild family. Over the years it has grown in population from 464 (in 1891) to 8,700 (in 1930) and 124,000 (in 1983).

Gederah

Town, south of Rehovot. Founded in 1884 by young members of the "Bilu" movement from Russia as a Moshavah (village). It was not dependent upon Baron Rothschild's aid or administration. Its population – 6,600 in the year 1983.

Zikhron-Ya'akov

Village on the southern spur of Mount Carmel, founded in 1882 by Jews from Rumania, members of the Hovevei Zion movement. The Rothschild family took a personal interest in the village, and grapevines were planted on their initiative.

Today the Zikhron wine cellars are famous for their excellent wines and spirits.

Rosh-Pinah

Moshavah in upper Galilee, founded in 1878 by Jews of Zefat (Safed), who left two years later. In 1882 it was resettled by newcomers of the "First Aliyah", Jewish pioneers from Rumania.

The population of the settlement rose from 350 following the establishment of the State of Israel to 1200 in 1983.

Der Judenstaat

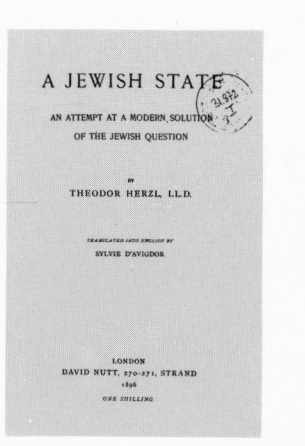

English edition

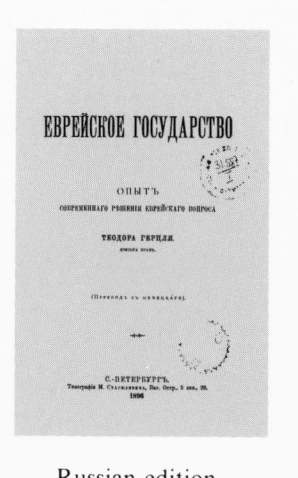

French edition

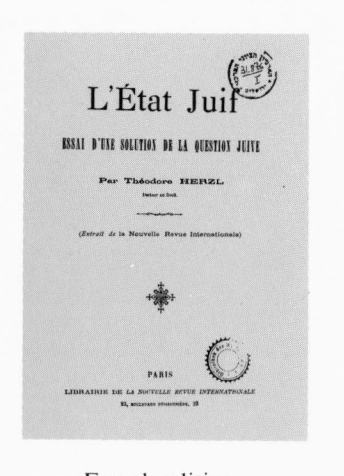

Russian edition

Portuguese edition

Hebrew edition, Warsaw

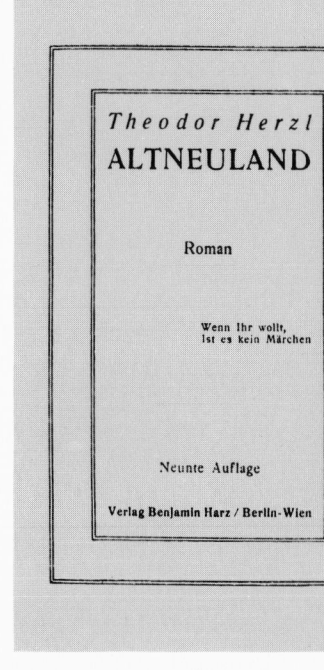

Title page of "Der Judenstaat", 1896

Altneuland

English edition

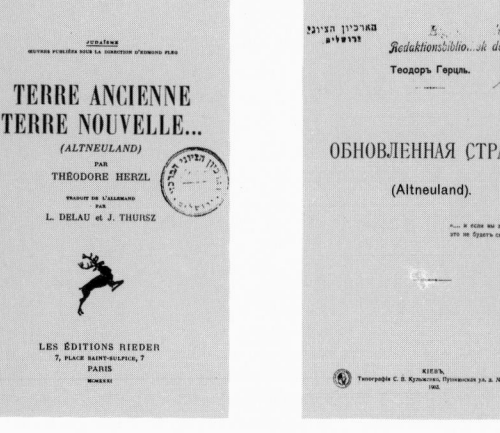

French edition

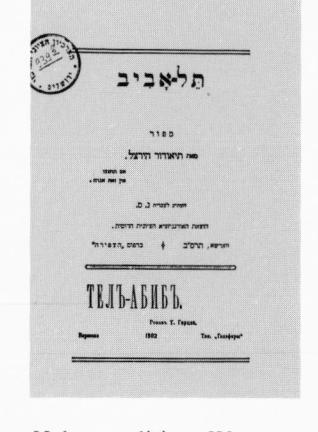

Russian edition

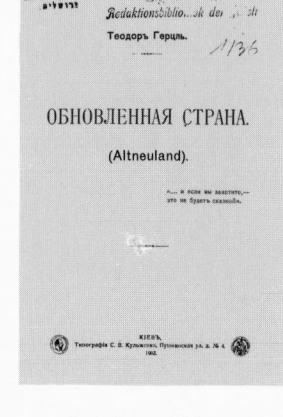

Hebrew edition, Warsaw

Hebrew edition, Tel Aviv

Title page of "Altneuland", 1902

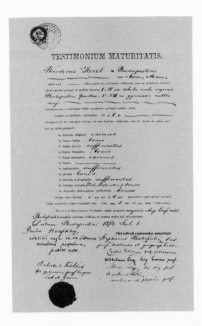

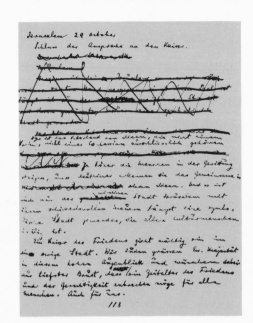

Dr. Th. Herzl's Certificate
of Matriculation, 1878.

Page from the diary of Dr. Th. Herzl,
on his encounter with the Kaiser.

Dr. Th. Herzl's authorization as delegate to the IV Congress.

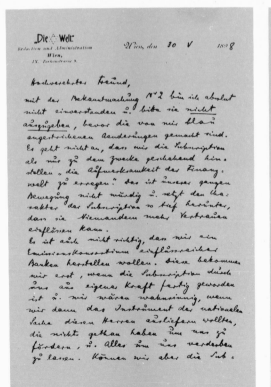

Letter by Dr. Th. Herzl
with his proposed flag for the Jewish State.

Dr. Th. Herzl's authorization as delegate to the VI Congress.

"... what the soil of our homeland is to our economic and physical lives – the Bible is to our spiritual and moral existence.

The Bible, held sacred also by hundreds of millions of non-Jews, bears eternal witness to the unshakable and unseverable link between the People of Israel and the Land of Israel..."

David Ben Gurion